# FUNCTIONAL PROGRAMMING WITH

# Miranda

## IAN HOLYER

Department of Computer Science
University of Bristol

PITMAN
PUBLISHING

PITMAN PUBLISHING
128 Long Acre, London WC2E 9AN

A Division of Longman Group UK Limited

First published in Great Britain 1991
Reprinted 1992 (twice)
Reprinted 1993

**British Library Cataloguing in Publication Data**
Holyer, Ian
   Functional programming with Miranda.
   I. Title
   005.362

   ISBN 0-273-03453-7

Reproduced and printed by photolithography
in Great Britain by Bell and Bain Ltd, Glasgow

Miranda
is a trademark of Research Software Ltd.

# Contents

# Preface

This book is aimed both at students and at professional programmers. It introduces not just a programming language, but also a style of programming – the declarative style – in which less emphasis is put on programming detail and more on problem solving than with traditional languages. The early chapters describe the methods used by functional programmers to design both small and large programs. The later chapters provide a non-mathematical introduction to the implementation and theory of functional languages.

The Miranda[1] language is described and used throughout most of the book. It is a simple language which nevertheless contains all the key features of functional languages and it has a good program development environment. It is used extensively for teaching and academic research, and is also increasingly being used in industrial applications.

The Miranda functional programming system is a product of Research Software Limited. I am grateful to Research Software Limited for permission to include information about the Miranda system in this book. However, this book does not aim to provide a detailed definition of the Miranda language, or its programming environment. An online reference manual is supplied with the system and this should be consulted for a complete description. The information given here is based on Miranda *release two*[2].

Thanks are due to David Turner for reading and commenting on a draft of this book. Thanks also go to Simon Peyton Jones, Gareth Waddell, David Carter, Neil Davies and Gill Rollings for their helpful comments, to a large number of Bristol University students for acting as guinea pigs, to Bristol University's Computer Science Department for its equipment and support, to Richard Stallman, Donald Knuth, Leslie Lamport and others for Gnu Emacs and LaTeX, the editing and typesetting packages used to create this book, and to my wife Judy for providing a fine example by diligently pursuing her own career.

---

[1] Miranda is a trademark of Research Software Ltd.

[2] Enquiries about the availability of the Miranda system should be addressed to Research Software Limited, 23 St Augustines Road, Canterbury CT1 1XP, England, or to the electronic mail address – "mira-request@ukc.ac.uk".

# Chapter 1

# Functional Languages

What are functional programming languages? There are hundreds of computer languages, with thousands of dialects, and they are not easy to classify, but the following diagram illustrates the connections between functional languages and their most important relatives:

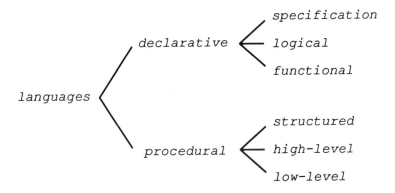

Functional languages belong to the **declarative** family, which also includes logic programming languages and specification languages, and this family is radically different from the more common **procedural** family.

## 1.1  Procedural Languages

The first procedural languages emerged in the early 1950s and most currently popular languages are procedural. Procedural languages all share two common ideas. The first is the idea of the execution of a sequence of instructions one after the other. The second is the idea of memory cells in which values are stored. These ideas are combined by defining procedures –

1

sequences of instructions which change the contents of memory cells. This is often summarised by saying that procedural languages are based on assignment, since assignments are the most fundamental instructions for updating memory cells.

The advantage of procedural languages, and the main reason for their popularity, is that they closely match the way in which most computers work, since the processor in a computer obeys sequences of machine code instructions which alter data stored in memory. However, this is also the main disadvantage of procedural languages, because it means that programmers have to deal with many details of storage, representation, manipulation and sequencing which have little to do with the problems they are trying to solve.

Within the procedural family, there has been an evolution from low level languages such as machine codes and assembly languages, through the so-called high level languages such as Fortran and Basic, to structured languages such as C and Pascal. This evolution has produced languages which are quite expressive and which free the programmer from many of the most mundane tasks.

## 1.2   Declarative Languages

Declarative languages have only been used for serious programming since the 1970s, although their origins can be traced back much further. Declarative languages attempt to lift programming to a higher level still by breaking away from the procedural model of programming completely, producing languages which allow algorithms to be expressed in very clear and direct ways, and which free the programmer almost completely from unnecessary details. They provide facilities for values to be defined and manipulated directly, without regard to where or how they are stored. Algorithms are expressed by declaring static relationships between values, without regard to the order in which these relationships need to be used in order to produce results.

All declarative languages make extensive use of **expressions** to declare relationships between values. Expressions are also very familiar tools in procedural languages, and so they form a good introduction to the ideas behind declarative programming. For example, in the procedural assignment:

$$x \quad := \quad a + b * c + d$$

the expression on the right hand side declares the value which is to be stored in the memory cell called $x$, without explicitly specifying the order in which the operations are to be performed, or how the intermediate values are to be computed and stored. Of course, the usual precedence conventions implicitly determine that the multiplication has to be done before the additions. A compiler can quite easily convert the assignment into a sequence of more primitive assignments by choosing an explicit ordering of operations and explicit memory cells for holding intermediate values:

```
t1   :=   b * c
t2   :=   a + t1
x    :=   t2 + d
```

The diagram on page 1 shows three categories of declarative language. These have not evolved from each other, but rather have developed separately. Nevertheless, they are closely related.

In functional languages, relationships are declared between values by defining **functions**. For example, a squaring function can be defined by:

```
square n  =  n * n
```

This expresses the relationship between the input value *n* and the output value *square n*. Language conventions ensure that such a function definition also specifies an algorithm for computing the output value from the input value, so that a compiler can convert the definition into a sequence of instructions.

Logic programming languages, most of which are dialects of Prolog, declare relationships between values using **relations**. For example, a relation *square* which specifies that one value is the square of another might be expressed in Prolog as:

```
square(N,M)   :-  M is N * N.
```

Relations differ from functions because a function produces a unique result value, whereas a relation can be used to express problems which may have no solution, or many solutions. For example, the definition:

```
parent(X,Y)   :-  mother(X,Y); father(X,Y).
```

can be used to express the relation that *Y* is a parent of *X*. Although *Y* is not uniquely determined from *X*, language conventions ensure that such a definition specifies an algorithm for searching for solutions (in this case, search for a mother, and if that fails, search for a father).

Specification languages such as VDM or Z are not programming languages as such, but rather languages in which to give precise specifications of tasks to be performed by computer. They usually use stylised mathematical notations, adapted for use in computational problems. They are more general than functional and logic languages because they allow relationships between values to be specified in ways which do not allow direct algorithms or search algorithms to be derived. For example, a sorting task which takes distinct values $x_1, \ldots, x_n$ and sorts them to produce $y_1, \ldots, y_n$ could be specified by

$$\{y_1, \ldots, y_n\} = \{x_1, \ldots, x_n\} \ \& \ \forall j \in \{1, \ldots, n-1\} \, y_j \le y_{j+1}$$

The idea is to begin with an indirect, mathematical description of the problem to be solved, to check that it is sound, to produce a practical implementation and to prove that it satisfies the specification. Some specification languages have executable subsets, and these subsets usually closely resemble functional or logic languages.

The emphasis in functional languages is on the clear expression of algorithms. The emphasis in logic languages is on knowledge bases and the deduction of logical consequences from them. The emphasis in specification languages is on agreeing and checking overall designs of large programming projects. Nevertheless, declarative languages all have the aims of making the programming of traditional applications easier and better controlled, and of providing features which allow new applications to be developed more easily.

## 1.3   Programming with Functions

Functional languages only emerged as serious programming languages in the 1980s, although hybrid languages such as Lisp which combine functional and procedural features have been popular since the 1950s.

The Miranda[1] language, which is described in the next chapter and used throughout most of this book, was developed in the mid 1980s primarily as a teaching and prototyping tool. It emphasizes simplicity and ease of program development. It is also being used increasingly in industry, and optimising compilers are being developed for it. Many other functional languages have been designed for various purposes, and a few of these are described briefly in Chapter 9.

---

[1] Miranda is a trademark of Research Software Limited

In this section, the main distinctive features of pure functional languages are described. These allow complete practical programming languages to be based on the use of pure functions, with no procedural features whatever.

## 1.3.1  Combining Functions

Functional languages are so called because functions are the basic building blocks from which programs are constructed, as we shall see in Chapter 3. A function is a self-contained unit which takes arguments and returns a result. In fact a complete program is regarded as a function from its input to its output:

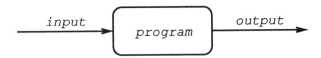

Picturing a function as a self-contained box with the arguments as the only information going in and the result as the only information coming out emphasises two properties of pure functions which distinguish them from procedures.

First, functions have no **side-effects**, that is they have no effect on the outside world other than to produce a result value. They cannot change global variables, or do any input or output other than through their arguments and results.

Second, functions have no **state**, that is they give the same result every time they are called with the same arguments – they have no internal memory of the history of their use. For example, you cannot write a function which produces a different random number every time it is called. A random number generator can, however, be written as a function which is called once and which returns a stream of numbers, as we shall see in Chapter 3.

These restrictions mean that functions form self-contained units – all their connections with the outside world are explicit. This makes them safe and convenient building blocks. Small-scale functions can be put together to form larger-scale functions, and many of the features of functional languages are designed to make it easy to build programs up in this way.

The most obvious way of combining functions is to pass the result value produced by one function call as an argument to a second function call. For example, a number can be taken to the fourth power by squaring it twice:

```
fourth_power n  =  square (square n)
```

Functions can also be combined by passing them as arguments to other functions, or returning them as results. For example, a function *squares* which squares each member of a list of numbers *ns* can be defined by:

    squares ns  =  map square ns

The expression *squares [1,2,3,4]* would yield the result *[1,4,9,16]*. The function *map* is a standard one taking two arguments. The first is a function and the second is a list. The given function is applied to each member of the given list to form a new list.

Functions such as *map* which take other functions as arguments, or which return functions as results, are often called **higher order** functions. This ability to pass function values around almost as if they were data values can be very powerful. For example, one of the language features which, in the past, has been thought essential for artificial intelligence applications is the ability for a program to change itself as it runs. This is one of the main features of Lisp, and has been carried over into logic programming languages such as Prolog. Functional languages do not allow this, but the ability to pass around function values can be used in its place, and indeed for many purposes it is a cleaner, safer and more controllable mechanism.

### 1.3.2  Laziness

The feature which, perhaps above all, makes it possible to define a complete programming language using only pure functions, with no procedural features whatever, is laziness. To see what this means, imagine an interactive program which asks questions to which the user gives answers. The answers which the user provides form the input to the program, and the questions which the program asks form the output. This leads to a rather curious situation if the program is pictured as a function:

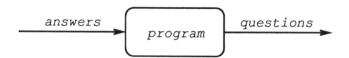

The function must produce the first part of its result (i.e. output the first question) before it reads in its argument (inputs any answers), and in general must alternate between producing parts of the result and reading in parts of the argument.

This does not fit in with the usual idea of function application in which arguments are evaluated before being passed to a function. Instead, a function calling mechanism is used in which unevaluated expressions are passed as arguments to the function, and it is regarded as the function's responsibility to evaluate those expressions as and when their values are needed. This is called **lazy** evaluation, because the evaluation of any expression is delayed as long as possible, and indeed if its value is never needed in order to produce a result, then it is never evaluated at all. Moreover, if the expression represents a compound data value, then it will only be evaluated to the extent needed to produce the result, and may contain embedded subexpressions which never get evaluated. This evaluation mechanism will be described in more detail in Section 2.6, and in Chapter 7.

Laziness solves the problem of the interactive program above, because the program is passed an unevaluated expression representing the stream of answers supplied by the user. The first question does not depend on these answers, and so can be output without any evaluation. Then the expression is evaluated enough to cause the first answer to be input, with the subexpression representing the rest of the answers remaining unevaluated. The second question can now be output, and so on. All the evaluation steps are demand driven, i.e. they are carried out in direct response to the need to print out results.

As well as making interactive input and output possible in a pure language, lazy evaluation brings other benefits, one of which is the ability to manipulate infinite data structures. This can often simplify programming problems. For example, it is very simple and natural to define the prime numbers, or the output from a random number generator, as an infinite list of numbers. Only those numbers which are actually needed to produce results get evaluated.

### 1.3.3 Polymorphic Types

The strict type rules of languages such as Pascal help greatly in ensuring that programs are correct by catching many errors during compilation. Moreover, they help the compiler to perform optimisations. However, these type systems are rather restrictive, as they only allow procedures to take one type of argument. For example, it is not possible to write a general sorting procedure – you have to write one procedure for numbers, another for strings, etc.

An alternative is to have no type rules, so that all values are treated equally, and all checking of types is done when programs are run rather than when they are compiled, as in most dialects of Prolog. This gives you the flexibility to be able to write general packages, but doesn't have the advantage of catching errors during compilation.

Many functional languages have what is called a **polymorphic** type system. Such a system has many different types, as with Pascal, and types are completely checked by the compiler. However, functions are allowed to take a variety of types under suitable circumstances. For example, the *map* function mentioned above can take any type of function as its first argument, but the type system ensures that its second argument is always a list of values, each of which is of the type which the given function expects. This type system makes it easy and natural to write truly general-purpose functions.

Another feature of the type system is that it is unobtrusive. No types need to be declared, as they do with Pascal. The compiler can deduce the types of functions directly from their definitions, and so type declarations need only be used for debugging or documentation purposes.

## 1.4   Advantages and Disadvantages

The main advantage of functional languages is that they allow algorithms to be expressed with clarity and brevity. Universities and colleges are increasingly teaching them to undergraduates as a first language, or alongside a procedural language, as an introduction to computing in which programming details can be kept to a minimum. Functional languages also form a useful introduction to other declarative languages.

Functional languages provide a very high level programming environment which is suitable for prototyping and experimental programming. One of the most important current uses of functional languages is in the rapid development of prototype programs. A functional program is typically several times shorter than an equivalent procedural one, and so is much quicker and easier to write, to debug, to adapt and to maintain. As optimising compilers emerge for functional languages, they are also becoming more and more widely used for large scale application programming.

Functional languages, because of their lack of unnecessary detail and their clean conventions, are also mathematically tractable and very suitable for program proof, transformation etc. In this book, we shall not say much about this aspect of functional programming, but readers who are interested in proofs will find good accounts in Bird & Wadler [5] and R. Turner [18].

Another advantage is that functional languages are not inherently sequential, so that both sequential and parallel algorithms can be expressed, and this means that functional languages are very suitable for use on parallel computers as well as sequential ones.

The main disadvantages of functional languages at their current state of development are the problems of availability, interfacing and efficiency.

At the time of writing, Miranda is the only pure functional language known to the author which is easily available and commercially supported on large computers, and there are no easily available languages on personal computers. However, functional languages are now widespread in academic circles, and it is only a matter of time before they become more widely available.

Current functional languages often do not provide good interfaces to external facilities such as graphics, databases or the operating system. This is partly because such external facilities are at present provided only in procedural form, for example as procedure libraries. However, it is possible to provide reasonably clean interfaces between functional programs and these external facilities, and research is being carried out in this area.

Efficiency problems come from several sources. First, many current implementations use interpreters rather than compilers, and so are much slower than one might hope for. There are already good compilers available for research purposes, and these are starting to become available commercially too. The version of Miranda on which this book is based uses a semi-interpretive system, but a full compiler is planned for the next version.

Second, higher level languages always tend to be a little less efficient than lower level ones. Compiler optimisations help keep this effect to a minimum, and a lot of research is being done on optimisation for functional language compilers.

Third, functional languages often do not have updatable data structures such as arrays (or have them grafted on as a procedural feature, forming a hybrid language). This is quite acceptable in a prototyping or teaching language, since arrays are not needed for prototype programming, and the declarative style of programming can be taught better without them. However, arrays (or some equivalent) are needed for efficiency reasons in large scale application programs. Arrays can be included in pure functional languages and are discussed further in Sections 4.7 and 6.5.3.

## 1.5 Structure of the Book

The first five chapters concentrate on the design of functional programs, providing a framework of ideas which functional programmers can use when problem solving. In Chapter 2, the Miranda language is introduced. Chapter 3 describes the design of small scale function definitions, Chapter 4 describes how these are built into modules, and Chapter 5 describes how modules in turn are put together to form larger programs.

Chapters 6 and 7 cover the main ideas behind compiling functional programs to give programmers a greater insight into the way a functional language works, and thus help them to make the best use of the language. The run-time system is covered in Chapter 7 in some detail, as this is where recently developed optimising compilers differ from more traditional interpreters or semi-interpretive systems. Chapter 8 is an informal introduction to the background mathematics of domains, on which the theory of functional languages is based. Chapter 9 contains a brief summary of a few functional languages other than Miranda – ones which represent some important turning points in the theory or practice of functional programming.

# Chapter 2

# Miranda

In this chapter, the core features of the Miranda language are introduced. Miranda is not a very large language, and most of the features are representative of those found in pure functional languages generally.

The programming environment provided by the Miranda system is introduced in the first section, and this is followed by descriptions of the basic data types, the structured data types and the definition and use of functions. The type system and evaluation mechanism used in pure functional languages are explained, and finally we give a few hints on programming style.

Language features connected with modules will be dealt with in Chapter 4, and the more advanced input and output features will be left until Chapter 5. Nevertheless, this chapter provides enough information for writing most simple programs.

## 2.1  The Programming Environment

The Miranda system provides not only a language in which to write programs but also an environment in which to develop them. Although this book is primarily about the language, all the examples are designed to be tried out directly within the programming environment, so it helps to have an outline understanding of the way in which the environment works.

Once you have given the command to enter the Miranda system, say *mira*, you can do all your program development within the system. After printing a sign-on message, Miranda will give a prompt. The prompt is the word *Miranda*, but we will use *?* as an abbreviation for it. At this prompt, you can type either an expression or a command. If you type an

expression, it is evaluated and its value printed out. The simplest use of the
Miranda system is to evaluate expressions in this way as if you were using
a calculator:

```
?   2+2
4
```

While in the system, there is always a current **script**. This is a file containing definitions and declarations written in the Miranda language. The
system provides a number of commands to manipulate scripts. The most
important one is the */edit* command which starts up an editor (one of the
ones provided on your computer) to allow you to edit the current script.
When you exit from the editor, the Miranda system will automatically compile the script and then give another prompt. The definitions in the script
are then available for use in evaluating expressions. For example, if the
current script contains the definitions:

```
ten   =   10
square n   =   n*n
```

then expressions involving the value *ten* and the function *square* can be
evaluated. For example:

```
?   6 + square (ten-4)
42
```

The ability to evaluate an arbitrary expression at any stage of development provides a powerful way of testing and debugging programs. A
program consists of a single script or a number of related scripts, and is
usually run from within the Miranda system by making its main script the
current one and then evaluating a suitable result expression. There are facilities for converting a program into an executable command, as with other
languages, but these facilities depend on the computer on which the system
is run – see the Miranda system manual for details.

In addition to commands for evaluating expressions and manipulating
scripts, the Miranda system provides a library of **standard functions** which
are available for use in all expressions and scripts. The main ones which are
used in this book are summarised in Appendix B. For convenience, Miranda's
operators are also summarised in this appendix. For full details see the
Miranda system manual.

## 2.2 Basic Data

There are three types of basic data in Miranda: numbers, booleans and characters. Numbers have type *num* and include both integers and floating point numbers. The booleans are the logical values *False* and *True*, and have type *bool*. Characters include all the letters, digits, punctuation, control characters etc. which can be typed on the keyboard, and have type *char*. For information about the type system and how to check what type a particular value has, see Section 2.5.

### 2.2.1 Numbers

Integers are written in the usual way, e.g. *123456*. There is no limit on the size of an integer (except that your program may run out of memory space). Floating point numbers are written with a decimal point or an exponent or both. For example *1.2*, *0.12e1* and *12e-1* all represent the same number – the *e* means "...times ten to the power...". Floating point numbers are approximate – they are stored to a fixed precision, usually about seventeen significant figures, though these may not all be displayed. For example:

```
?  pi
3.14159265359
```

The standard operators *+*, *-*, *\**, *\/* and *^* work on integers or floating point numbers. The minus sign *-* is used both as a prefix negation operator as in *-n*, and as an infix subtraction operator as in *n-1*. It is always treated as subtraction if possible. For example, *f -1* is taken to mean subtraction of *1* from *f*, so you have to write *f (-1)* to mean the application of *f* to *-1*. Multiplication always has to be done explicitly with the *\** operator, as in *m\*n*, as the expression *mn* represents a single two-letter identifier. The *^* operator is used for powers, e.g. *m^n* means *m* to the power *n*. These operators have the usual precedences; *^* binds tighter than *\** and *\/*, which bind tighter than *+* and *-*, so for example *6+4\*3^2* means *6+(4\*(3^2))*, as Miranda will verify:

```
?   6+4*3^2
42
```

The operators *+*, *-* and *\** return integers if given integers, but the division operator *\/* always returns a floating point number. If integers and floating point numbers are mixed, as in *2/3.4*, then integers are automatically converted into floating point form. The standard operators **div** and *mod* are provided for integer division and remainder. They only accept integer arguments, as with many other functions and operators, and even floating point numbers such as *2.0* which appear to be integral will not do. There is a standard function *integer* which tests whether a number is an integer or not, so this can be demonstrated by evaluating an expression:

```
?  integer 2.0
False
```

When floating point numbers need to be converted into integers, this has to be done explicitly with the standard function *entier* which discards the fractional part of a number:

```
?  entier (2+3.4)
5
```

There are many more standard numerical functions such as *abs*, *sqrt*, *sin* and *log*, together with some standard numbers such as *pi* and *e*. For more details on the standard operators and functions and their effects, consult the Miranda system manual (available interactively via the command */man*) or just experiment by evaluating expressions as above.

### 2.2.2  Booleans

The boolean values, which are of type *bool*, are *False* and *True*, and the standard boolean operators are & (and), \/ (or) and ~ (not), together with the comparison operators =, ~=, <, >, <= and >=. The comparison operators bind tighter than ~ which binds tighter than & which binds tighter than \/. If in doubt, use parentheses. As a useful shorthand, comparison operators can be chained so that, for example, $m<n<p$ is short for $m<n$ & $n<p$.

The boolean operators & and \/ never evaluate their second arguments unnecessarily. For example, a function *invertible* to test whether a number remains the same when inverted can be defined by:

```
invertible n  =  n~=0 & 1/n=n
```

The function returns *False* when n is *0*, despite the fact that the second argument *1/n=n* of & would cause an error if it were evaluated. This is an example of the general principle of laziness explained in Section 2.6.

### 2.2.3 Characters

Characters, of type *char*, are written with single quotes (apostrophes), as in *'a'*, and include all the usual characters you can type on a keyboard – upper and lower case letters, digits, operator symbols such as *'+'* and punctuation marks such as *','*. Also included are the invisible control characters, of which the most important is *'\n'* which is the **newline** character, the one usually entered into the computer by pressing the key marked RETURN or ENTER. All the control characters have names which start with the character \ and the character \ itself has to be written *'\\'*. There are no standard operators for characters, though they can be compared with the comparison operators (as can all non-function types – see Section 2.5):

```
?   'a' < 'z'
True
```

There are standard functions *code* and *decode*, which convert characters to and from the numerical codes which are used to represent them in the computer. For example, the expression *code 'a'* gives the result *97* (on most computers). There are also standard functions *letter* and *digit* which test whether a character is a letter or a digit.

## 2.3 Structured Data

There are three ways in which structured data can be built up from components. Values can be combined into lists, tuples, or structures. **Lists** are sequences or streams of values, all of the same type. The type of a list depends on the type of its members; the type of a list of numbers is *[num]*, of a list of booleans is *[bool]*, and so on. **Tuples** contain a fixed number of items of different types. The type of a tuple depends on the number and type of the items in it. For example, *(num,bool,char)* is the type of triples containing a number, a boolean and a character. **Structures** are similar to tuples in some ways, but provide more flexibility. They allow new programmer defined types to be introduced, they allow alternative representations for values of a single type, and they allow recursive types to be defined for representing such things as trees. For more information about the types of structured data values, see Section 2.5.

## 2.3.1   Lists

List processing plays a prominent part in functional programming, and so Miranda has many facilities for handling lists. A list is an ordered collection of items. It can contain any number of members, and can even be infinite, as long as all the members have the same type. Lists are normally processed sequentially by running through their members in order.

A list can be represented with square brackets and commas, for example *[2,4,6]*, and indeed Miranda usually prints list values out in this style. The empty list is written *[]*, and arbitrarily complicated expressions can be used to specify the members of non-empty lists:

```
?   [1+1,2*2,3^3]
[2,4,27]
```

Such direct representations can be used for finite lists whose length is known and where there is an explicit expression for each member. There are also several other convenient notations for lists, namely ranges, string constants and list comprehensions.

Ranges are provided as a notation for lists of consecutive numbers. A **range** is an expression of the form *[m..n]* representing all the numbers from *m* up to *n* inclusive in steps of *1*. There is also a form *[m0,m1..n]* in which the first two members are specified, allowing for a stepsize other than *1*. In either form, the limit *n* can be left out to indicate an infinite list. For example, the list of all odd numbers can be generated by:

```
?   [1,3..]
[1,3,5,7,9,11,13,15,        (this continues indefinitely)
```

If you try this, the evaluation will continue until you interrupt it with the interruption mechanism provided on your computer (often holding down the CONTROL key and typing C).

Miranda has an extra notation for lists of characters. They can be written as **string constants** using double quotes (speech marks). For example, the string *"abc"* is an abbreviation for the list of characters *['a','b','c']*. The two notations are interchangeable, so all general list operators and functions can be used on string constants. String constants can contain control characters as well as visible characters, so for example a two-line piece of text can be represented by the string constant *"1st line\n2nd line\n"* with the newline character *'\n'* at the end of each line.

Miranda prints lists of characters in a different way from other lists. It prints the characters in the list directly, without surrounding quotes, and in such a way that control characters have their proper effect. This is so that programs can be written to output any desired stream of characters. For example:

```
?   "1st line\n2nd line\n"
1st line
2nd line
```

This special treatment only occurs if the result expression itself is a list of characters. If the result expression contains a list of characters embedded in some larger data structure, then the list is printed as a string constant:

```
?   ["1st line\n2nd line\n"]
["1st line\n2nd line\n"]
```

A **list comprehension** is a special notation for lists in which a list is specified in terms of generators and filters. The notation is based on the conventions used in mathematics for specifying sets. For example, the list of squares of the even numbers between $1$ and $10$ can be found by:

```
?   [n^2 | n<-[1..10]; n mod 2 = 0]
[4,16,36,64,100]
```

The vertical bar / can be read "such that", and the generator symbol <- (which is made up from a less than sign and a minus sign and looks a little like the mathematical symbol $\in$) can be read "is taken from" or "runs through". Thus the list above can be read "the list of $n\char`\^2$ such that $n$ is taken from *[1..10]* and $n$ **mod** $2$ is $0$".

In general, the vertical bar can be followed by any number of generators and filters, separated by semicolons. Each generator introduces a new local variable which can be used in subsequent generators and filters, and in the expression before the vertical bar. Each filter is a condition which cuts down the number of items generated.

We will see in Section 2.4.3 that patterns can be used as well as variable names in generators. Various ways in which list comprehensions can be used as a powerful tool in designing function definitions will be described in the next chapter.

The standard operators on lists are the : operator which adds a new member to the front of a list, the ++ operator which joins (concatenates) two

lists, the prefix operator # which finds the length of a list, the *!* operator
which extracts the *n*th member of a list, and the less often used *--* operator
which subtracts one list from another.

The *:* operator can be used to construct lists member by member. For
example, if *n* is a number and *ns* is a list of numbers, then *n:ns* is a longer
list obtained from *ns* by adding *n* to the front. Thus a list of length *3*
containing the numbers *2*, *4* and *6* in that order could be written *2:4:6:[]*,
which is short for *2:(4:(6:[]))*. This has exactly the same meaning as
*[2,4,6]*:

```
    ?   [2,4,6] = 2:4:6:[]
    True
```

Perhaps the most important use of the *:* operator is in patterns (see Section 2.4) to break a list down into its **head** (first member) and **tail** (list of
remaining members). This can be done repeatedly in order to work through
the list.

The *++* operator is used very frequently for joining lists together:

```
    ?   [2,4,6] ++ [1,3,5,7]
    [2,4,6,1,3,5,7]
```

However, since lists are implemented in a similar way to linked lists in procedural languages (see Chapter 7), the *++* operator is efficient only if its first
argument is short – it usually makes a copy of the first list before attaching
the second to the end. This inefficiency is not important for single uses of
the operator, but needs to be taken into account when it is used repeatedly,
particularly in general purpose modules (see Chapter 4).

The *!* operator acts rather like array indexing – the expression *xs!n*
extracts the *n*th member of the list *xs*, where the numbering of the members
starts from *0*. However, it does not take constant time as array indexing
does, because the list has to be scanned. Thus the *!* operator should be
used sparingly – in particular, it should definitely not be used to run through
the members of a list by forming *xs!0*, *xs!1* etc. in turn.

There are many standard functions provided for processing lists, some
of which will be described in detail in the next chapter. For example, the
function call *map f xs* applies a function *f* to each member of a list *xs* to
form a new list, *filter f xs* forms a list from those members of *xs* which
pass a test *f* (i.e. for which the function *f* returns *True*) and *concat xss*
joins a collection of lists end to end:

```
? concat ["prog","ram","ming"]
programming
```

The function call *take n xs* forms a list from the first *n* members of *xs*, and the call *takewhile f xs* forms a list from those members at the beginning of *xs* which pass a test represented by a function *f*. There are similar functions *drop* and *dropwhile*. There are functions *hd* and *tl* for extracting the head and tail of a list, and *member* for testing whether a list contains a particular value. The functions *reverse* and *sort* are used for reversing and sorting lists:

```
? sort ["a","bee","and","an","ant"]
["a","an","and","ant","bee"]
```

In addition to such general purpose functions which work on any type of list, there are standard functions for handling lists of particular types. For example, *sum* and *product* work on lists of numbers, *and* and *or* work on lists of booleans, *cjustify* and *lay* work on lists of characters.

The wide variety of standard notations and functions on lists often leads to several different ways of producing the same result. In order to become familiar with the standard functions on lists, and to find out about others which have not been mentioned here, you should look through the list of standard functions in Appendix B, as well as going through the exercises at the end of this chapter.

## 2.3.2 Tuples

The word tuple is a general term covering pairs, triples, quadruples, quin-tuples, sextuples etc. A tuple contains a number of **fields** which can be of different types. However, the fields do not have names, and cannot be altered individually in the way that fields can in procedural languages.

Tuples are written with parentheses and commas, for example *(3,6)* or *(5,'x',True)*. The standard functions *fst* and *snd* extract the first and second components of a pair – there are no standard functions for tuples of other lengths, though they can be defined easily if needed. The standard function *zip2* takes two lists and forms a list of corresponding pairs. For example, *zip2 [1,2,3] "abc"* returns the list *[(1,'a'), (2,'b'), (3,'c')]*.

One of the main uses of tuples is in defining functions which return several values rather than just one. For example, a function *roots* which finds the two roots of a quadratic equation with coefficients *a*, *b* and *c* might have a definition of the form:

```
roots a b c  =  (r1,r2)  where  ...
```

Such a function is called by using a tuple on the left hand side of a definition which gives names to all the result values in one go:

```
(root1,root2)  =  roots ...
```

Another common use for tuples is to process the corresponding members of several lists. For example, the corresponding members of two lists of numbers can be added as follows:

```
?  [m+n | (m,n) <- zip2 [1,2,3] [4,5,6]]
[5,7,9]
```

It would not be correct to use two separate generators for $m$ and $n$ because that would generate all pairs, not just corresponding ones. Thus the two lists are combined into a single list of pairs with `zip2`, and then a single generator is used to give names to the two components of each pair in turn. Definitions and generators with tuples on the left are special cases of pattern matching which will be dealt with in Section 2.4.

### 2.3.3   Structures

A structure, like a tuple, contains a fixed number of fields of different types. Structures are created by introducing new programmer defined types, called **algebraic types**. For example, if you want to introduce structures for representing information about people, a new type `person` can be defined in a script:

```
person  ::=  Person [char] num sex
```

The symbol `::=` indicates that a new type is being defined. Values of this type are structures containing three fields of type `[char]`, `num` and `sex` (defined below) representing a person's name, age and sex. A person structure such as `Person "Sam" 18 Female` is very similar to a triple `("Sam", 18, Female)`. The most important difference is that `person` structures form a separate type and cannot be confused with any other structures with the same three field types.

In procedural languages, structures are processed by updating or extracting individual fields one at a time by name. As functional languages have no notion of a sequence of processing steps or of updating memory cells, the fields of a structure cannot be accessed individually in a direct way. Instead of individual field names, a structure has a **constructor** function which builds a new structure from its fields. In the above example, a new constructor *Person* was introduced as part of the type definition. Constructor names always begin with a capital letter and no other kinds of name begin with capitals.

Algebraic types allow alternative representations for values within the same type. In the example of the *roots* function above, not all quadratic equations have real roots, so it may be appropriate to introduce a special type *result* to represent the result returned by the function:

```
result   ::=   Success num num | Fail [char]
```

There are two alternatives separated by a vertical bar / indicating that a result is either a structure *Success r1 r2* containing the two roots, or else a structure such as *Fail "No real roots"* representing failure and containing an error message giving the reason.

In general, a type definition of this form can have any number of alternatives, each introducing a new constructor with any number of arguments, somewhat like "variant" or "union" structures in procedural languages. A value of the new type can be thought of as consisting of a small integer **tag** indicating which constructor is involved, followed by the relevant fields.

A constructor need have no fields at all, in which case it is just a constant. This gives us a way of introducing enumerated types. For example, the definitions:

```
sex   ::=   Female | Male
day   ::=   Mon | Tue | Wed | Thu | Fri | Sat | Sun
```

introduce new types *sex* consisting of two new constants and *day* consisting of seven new constants. These constants act like synonyms for small integers, except that you cannot do arithmetic on them or mix constants of different types.

An important property of the constructors introduced in algebraic types is that they can take part in pattern matching, as we shall see in Section 2.4. Another feature of algebraic types is that they can be polymorphic, i.e. the values can have components of arbitrary types in the same way as lists. This will be demonstrated in Section 2.5. Also, algebraic types can be recursive, i.e. the values can contain components of the same type as themselves. This is important in building data structures such as trees, as we shall see in Chapter 4.

It is a remarkable fact that algebraic type definitions can be used to define all the usual types met in programming languages. In particular, Miranda's built-in types act as if they were introduced in this way. For example, the empty list *[]* and the operator *:* are regarded as constructors for lists – the only difference is that lists have special syntax conventions associated with them. This fact helps to gain a uniform understanding of data values, as we shall see in Chapter 8.

## 2.4   Functions

Remarkably sophisticated problems can be solved by constructing one-line expressions and evaluating them interactively. However, serious programming is done by defining functions in a script. Functions and constant data values are defined by equations:

```
square n  =  n*n
fourth_power n  =  twice square n
twice f x  =  f (f x)
naturals  =  [0..]
multiples n  =  [n, n+n ..]
```

Each definition introduces a new **identifier**, i.e. a name for a data or function value. Identifiers must begin with a lower case letter – only constructors begin with capitals. Identifiers can contain upper or lower case letters, digits, underscores (as hyphens) and single quotes (as dashes).

The order of the definitions in a script is unimportant, and identifiers can be used before they are defined. The **scope** of the top-level identifiers such as *square* in the above example, i.e. the region in which they can be accessed, is the whole script. The **formal parameters** such as *n*, *f* and *x* which appear in equations are local – the scope of such a parameter is just the equation in which it appears. Parameters do not need to be declared – their appearance on the left hand side of an equation is sufficient, and their types are deduced automatically.

In function applications, the arguments are not normally surrounded by parentheses and commas as in other languages. In fact *f x y* is a function applied to two arguments, whereas *f (x,y)* is a function applied to one argument – a pair. Function application binds tighter than any operator, so *f x:ys* means *(f x):ys*. Function arguments which are compound expressions usually need parentheses, e.g. *f (x:ys)* or *f (-1)*.

In the rest of this section, we describe three special notations provided in Miranda which make function definitions more expressive. These are guards, local definitions, and patterns. We also present some important notations and conventions concerned with the higher order use of functions, i.e. the ability to pass functions as arguments, return them as results and store them in data structures.

## 2.4.1 Guards

In a **guarded equation**, the right hand side specifies a number of different result expressions, each accompanied by a guard, i.e. the condition under which that expression is to be returned. For example, the standard function *max2* which finds the maximum of two numbers (or values of other types) can be defined by:

```
max2 m n
 =   m,  if m > n
 =   n,  if m <= n
```

This is very similar to the *if ...then ...else ...* constructions of procedural languages – the guards are tested in turn to find out which result expression to return. If none of the guards apply, and there are no more defining equations for the function, a run-time error occurs. The last guard can be replaced by the word *otherwise* if it represents all possible remaining cases.

## 2.4.2 Local Definitions

A **local definition** is one introduced inside a **where** clause. Such a definition is only available for use inside the right hand side to which the *where* clause is attached. For example, a function to split a list into two roughly equal halves can be defined by:

```
split xs
 =  (take half xs, drop half xs)   where
     half  =  #xs div 2
```

This illustrates one of the reasons for using local definitions – to handle shared subexpressions. The local definition of *half* ensures that the subexpression *#xs div 2* is only evaluated once, despite the fact that it is used in two different places.

Local definitions can be added to guarded equations, in which case the definitions are available in all the clauses of the equation. For example, a

function *roots* which finds the real roots, if any, of a quadratic polynomial
*a\*x^2+b\*x+c* (i.e. the values of *x* which make it zero) from the coefficients
*a*, *b* and *c* can be written:

```
roots a b c
=  (r1,r2),                if d >= 0
=  error "no real roots",  otherwise
   where
   r1  =  (-b+r) / (2*a)
   r2  =  (-b-r) / (2*a)
   r  =  sqrt d
   d  =  b^2 - 4*a*c
```

As can be seen in this example, local definitions often depend on the formal
parameters of the main function.

### 2.4.3   Patterns

Another notation provided to enhance the expressibility of definitions is
pattern matching. A **pattern** is an expression made up from constructors
and formal parameters, and allows structured values to be broken down into
their components. For example, given the algebraic type *person* defined
in Section 2.3.3, functions which extract and use the fields of a *person*
structure can, for example, be defined by:

```
name (Person cs n s)  =  cs
age (Person cs n s)  =  n
adult (Person cs n s)  =  n >= 18
```

When one of these functions is called, the actual argument is matched
against the pattern *Person cs n s* and the local parameters *cs*, *n* and
*s* are set equal to its fields.

Several equations can be written down to define a single function, each
equation specifying a pattern which the arguments must match for that
equation to be used. As with guards, the equations are tried in order until
one matches (if any). For example, given the enumerated type *day* defined
in Section 2.3.3, a function to test whether a day is part of the weekend can
be written:

```
weekend Sat  =  True
weekend Sun  =  True
weekend d  =  False
```

The third equation matches when all the others fail, and so acts as a default case.

Guards and pattern matching can interact with each other. If none of the guards in an equation hold, then the next equation will be tried. For example, an alternative definition of the *weekend* function above is:

```
weekend d   =  False,   if ~member [Sat,Sun] d
weekend Sat =  True
weekend Sun =  True
```

Pattern matching can be used with the standard types as well as with programmer defined algebraic types. The *bool* and *char* types are treated as enumerated, so that all boolean and character constants can be used in pattern matching. With the type *num*, all integer constants are treated as constructors, and in addition the operators *(+1)*, *(+2)*, ...are treated as constructors for positive numbers, to make recursive definitions over the natural numbers more convenient. For example the factorial function *fac* can be written:

```
fac 0 = 1
fac (n+1)  =  (n+1) * fac n
```

Recursive function definitions, i.e. ones in which a function calls itself, will be described in some detail in the next chapter.

The tuple notations, *(,)* for pairs, *(,,)* for triples and so on, are regarded as constructors for tuples, so they too can be used in pattern matching. Where lists are concerned, *[]* and *:* are the constructors. Patterns such as *[]* and *(x:rxs)* are used to distinguish between empty and non-empty lists. The pattern *(x:rxs)* splits a list *xs* into its head and tail, i.e. the first member *x* and the list of remaining members *rxs*. For example, a function *length*, equivalent to the standard # operator, which finds the length of a list can be defined by:

```
length [] = 0
length (x:rxs)  =  1 + length rxs
```

A pattern can be an arbitrarily complicated expression built up from constructors and parameters and, in particular, list expressions with a fixed structure such as string constants can be used when matching lists. Any number of a function's arguments can be matched against patterns simultaneously. Patterns can also be used on the left hand side of definitions and in list comprehensions, which can be particularly useful when handling tuples. A few individual equations which provide examples of the possibilities are:

```
polite "please"  =  True
third (x1:x2:x3:rxs)  =  x3
thirds (x1:x2:x3:rxs) (y1:y2:y3:rys)  =  (x3,y3)
(lowerc,upperc)  =  thirds "abcdef" "ABCDEF"
addvectors ms ns  =  [m+n | (m,n) <- zip2 ms ns]
```

There will be many more examples of pattern matching in the following chapters.

### 2.4.4  Higher Order Functions

The main operation which you can perform on a function is to apply it. In functional languages, you can also pass functions as arguments and return them as results. For example, the dot operator *(.)* is a standard operator which forms the composition of two functions, so that *f.g* is a function *h* for which *h x* is equivalent to *f (g x)*. For example, *sqrt.abs* is a function for finding the square root of the absolute value of a number.

A function which acts on functions, i.e. which takes another function as one of its arguments or returns a function as its result, is called a **higher order** function. No special notation is needed to define higher order functions. For example, a function *compose* which is equivalent to the standard *(.)* operator can be defined by:

```
compose f g
=  h  where
    h x  =  f (g x)
```

Operators like + and * are just functions of two arguments with a special infix syntax. You can treat an operator as a function name by putting parentheses round it, e.g. *(+)*, to remove this special syntax, and then it becomes suitable for passing as an argument. For example, the standard function *map2* combines corresponding members of two lists with a given operation, so that *map2 (+) ms ns* can be used to add corresponding members of *ms* and *ns*.

As well as turning an operator into a normal function, you can also turn a normal function into an infix operator by putting a dollar *$* character in front of it. For example, the expressions *max2 m n* and *m $max2 n* are interchangeable.

An important feature of functional languages is the ability to form a **partial application** of a function to pass as an argument. An infix operator can be applied to either argument on its own to form a **section** – for example

*(/2)* is a halving function and *(1/)* is an inverting function. Functions with normal syntax can be applied just to their first argument, or first few arguments. For example, *map sqrt* is a function which, when applied to a list of numbers, forms a new list from the square roots.

The partial application feature is often called **currying** after the mathematician Haskell Curry. Any function can be regarded as being applied to its arguments one at a time. For example, the call *max2 m n* is regarded as being equivalent to *(max2 m) n*, i.e. the partial application *max2 m* applied to the argument *n*. It is important to understand this feature, even if only for debugging purposes – leaving out an argument by accident may produce a legitimate expression. The feature also ties in with functions being passed back as results. For example, the *compose* function above can alternatively be defined as a function of three arguments by:

```
compose f g x  =  f (g x)
```

The normal use of *compose* to combine two functions is then regarded as a partial application. Indeed, this definition and the previous one are completely interchangeable.

Constructors can also take functions as arguments, and so functions can be embedded in data structures. For example, it is possible to form a list of functions such as *[abs,sqrt,sin,exp]* provided they are all of the same type.

Higher order functions correspond roughly to the features found in some other languages, notably Lisp and Prolog, which allow programs to change themselves as they run, as mentioned in Section 1.3.1. Such features lend a great deal of expressive power to a language. The approach taken in functional languages is a very safe and controlled one – as functions have no side effects, they form self-contained program components which can be combined in well-defined ways through their arguments and results. Moreover, it is only the action of a function which is important in combining it – its structure, i.e. its definition, cannot be accessed. Functions are treated rather like abstract types (see Chapter 4) in which application is the only visible operation. This allows functions to be regarded as manipulable values, and a sound and self-consistent mathematical theory of them can be built as described in Chapter 8.

## 2.5 Types

Miranda is a strongly typed language – every function and data value has a type, and all the types in a program are checked by the compiler to ensure

that functions are never applied to arguments of the wrong type when the
program is run. If you give an expression followed by the symbol *::* then
Miranda will print out the type of the expression rather than evaluating it:

```
?   2+2 ::
num
```

The basic data types are *num*, *bool* and *char*. The type *num* includes
both integers and floating point numbers, so that these are normally compatible with each other. The type of a list such as *[1,2]* is *[num]* and
lists are compatible, regardless of length, if they have members of the same
type. The type of a tuple such as *(5, True)* is *(num, bool)*, so that tuples are only compatible if they have exactly the same number and types of
components. The type of a structure is the named type which introduces
its constructor, so for example the type of *Person* structures is *person*.

The type of a function with one argument such as the standard function
*digit* is *char->bool* indicating that it takes a character as argument and
returns a boolean as result. The type of a two-argument function such as
*(<)* is *num->num->bool* indicating that it takes two numbers and returns
a boolean. (Actually, *(<)* has a more general type – see Section 2.5.2.) The
*->* symbol is right associative so that *num->num->bool* is equivalent to
*num->(num->bool)*. This is consistent with the fact that *(<)* can be partially applied to a single argument, returning a function of type *num->bool*.
For example, *(0<)* is a function of type *num->bool* for testing whether a
number is positive.

The type system is quite unobtrusive. The types of functions need not
be specified – the compiler infers their types from their definitions. However,
it is good practice to specify the types of functions in scripts, in which case
the compiler checks that the specified type agrees with the inferred type.
The type of a function is specified separately from its definition, as in the
following definition of the function *rms* which finds the root mean square
of a list of numbers:

```
rms   ::   [num]->num

rms ns  =  sqrt (sum [n^2 | n<-ns] / #ns)
```

The inclusion of such type specifications is useful for documentation
purposes, particularly for library functions intended for use in other scripts,
for debugging purposes, or to restrict the type of a function to make it less
general. To make type specifications more readable, type synonyms can be
defined with the == symbol:

```
text  ==  [char]
```

The type system is a powerful one, allowing functions to be defined which act on a variety of different types. Two ways in which this can happen are described below – polymorphism and overloading. A polymorphic function acts on, say, a list with any type of members in a uniform way by processing only the structure of the list, so that the type of the members does not matter. An overloaded function acts in a less uniform way by processing different types in different ways.

## 2.5.1 Polymorphism

A **polymorphic** function is one which can be applied to arguments of different types at different times. For example, the *reverse* function can be applied to any type of list, returning a list of the same type. The *reverse* function has type *[*]->[*]*, where the type variable * stands for any particular type. A **type variable** is one of the symbols *, **, ***, ...made up from * characters. The only other functions having the polymorphic type *[*]->[*]* are ones such as *tl* or *init* which re-arrange the structure of a list in some way, without "looking inside" the members.

The compiler, in analysing the definition of a polymorphic function, is capable of determining the most general form of arguments to which the function can be applied. As another example, the function *map2* has the type:

$$(*->**->***) ->[*]->[**]->[***]$$

This has three type variables in it, each standing for a separate arbitrary type. The type indicates that *map2* takes an arbitrary two-argument function and two lists, and produces a list as result. The members of the three lists have types corresponding to the argument and result types of the given function.

Constructors can be polymorphic just as with ordinary functions. For example, the list constructor *:* has the polymorphic type *->[*]->[*]*, and it is this which determines the fact that lists can contain members of any type. Programmer defined structures can also be polymorphic. For example, a type for representing trees, which we shall meet in Chapter 4, can be defined by:

```
tree *  ::=  Tree * [tree *]
```

This defines a new polymorphic type *tree* * where * can be replaced by any type. Thus *tree num* would be a tree of numbers, *tree [char]* a tree of strings, etc. The new constructor *Tree* introduced by the definition is polymorphic. Its first field can be of any type, and its second is a list of subtrees of the same type.

## 2.5.2   Overloading

Sometimes, functions are needed which are defined over a variety of types, but which have different effects on different types, rather than just doing structural processing which is independent of type. Such functions are called **overloaded**. The polymorphic type system usually used in functional languages, including Miranda, cannot cope with overloading. Standard operators and functions can be overloaded using various tricks, but programmer defined functions cannot be overloaded. In the Haskell language (see Chapter 9), an experimental system of classes has been designed to allow a more uniform approach to overloading. There are several circumstances in which standard operators and functions are overloaded in Miranda.

First, arithmetic functions have to be able to work on both integers and floating point numbers, which are stored in different ways. Instead of making these separate types, as in other languages, they are treated as a single type in Miranda, with run-time tests being used to distinguish them where necessary.

Second, the comparison operators =, < and so on are defined on all data types. They are not truly polymorphic, because their meaning must depend on the type to which they are applied. However, a sensible ordering can be defined on every data type (other than functions and abstract data types). The ordering on basic types, such as numbers and characters, is as you would expect, and Miranda imposes an arbitrary but uniform ordering on data structures such as lists etc. The comparison operators can then be treated by the type system just as if they were polymorphic, of type *->*->bool*.

Third, the function *show* which converts a value into a string, e.g. to be printed, is also defined on all data types, in this case including functions and abstract types. Applying *show* to a function, for example, yields the string *"<function>"*. Again *show* is not truly polymorphic, because in reality there is a different show function for each type. However, because there is a complete collection of these functions, the type system can treat *show* as if it were a polymorphic function of type *->[char]*. For more details about *show* see the Miranda system manual.

## 2.6 Evaluation

In order to program well in any language, you need some mental picture of how the language works. In the case of procedural languages, the picture involves a sequence of instructions being executed, each instruction causing changes to the contents of memory cells, or changes to the execution sequence.

In functional languages, the code is made up of static function definitions, and running a program amounts to evaluating an expression. In this section, we describe a simple technique called reduction for evaluating expressions by hand. An actual implementation of a functional language can be regarded as an optimised variation on this technique, as we shall see in Chapter 7.

One of the most important features of the evaluation mechanism of a pure functional language like Miranda is that it is lazy, meaning that subexpressions are not evaluated unnecessarily – their evaluation is delayed until their values are actually required. One of the important consequences of lazy evaluation is that input and output can be implemented in a particularly simple way. The questions of laziness and of input and output are discussed below.

### 2.6.1 Laziness

In **reduction**, the expression to be evaluated is repeatedly re-written (reduced) by replacing some subexpression by an equivalent one until the expression is in **normal form**, i.e. a form in which no more processing is possible. This normal form is, essentially, the value of the expression and is printed out as the result of the evaluation.

At each reduction step, a subexpression is chosen for replacement. The subexpression usually consists of a function applied to some arguments, and is replaced by the result of calling the function. For example, suppose the current script contains the function definitions:

```
double n  =  n+n
square n  =  n*n
```

Then the evaluation of the expression *double (square (2+2) + 5)* can be carried out as follows. At each step, the subexpression which is about to be replaced is underlined:

```
?   double (square (2+2) + 5)
→   double (square 4 + 5)
```

```
→  double (4*4 + 5)
→  double (16+5)
→  double 21
→  21+21
→  42
```

Which subexpression should be chosen for replacement at each step? Various replacement strategies are possible, ranging between the two extremes of innermost and outermost evaluation. An **innermost** evaluation strategy is like the one shown above, where an innermost subexpression is chosen for replacement at each stage. This corresponds to evaluating all the arguments to a function before calling it. An **outermost** strategy corresponds to choosing an outermost replaceable subexpression at each step. The above example can be evaluated with an outermost strategy as follows:

```
?  double (square (2+2) + 5)
→  (square (2+2) + 5) + (square (2+2) + 5)
→  ((2+2)*(2+2) + 5) + ((2+2)*(2+2) + 5)
→  (4*4 + 5) + (4*4 + 5)
→  (16+5) + (16+5)
→  21+21
→  42
```

A function is called as soon as enough information about its arguments is available to make a replacement. Functions are called by passing unevaluated or partially evaluated expressions as arguments. This often causes multiple copies of a subexpression to be created. In the above example, these copies are shown as being evaluated together. In practical implementations, care needs to be taken to ensure that subexpressions are shared rather than copied for efficiency – see Section 6.5.2 and Chapter 7. This sharing can be represented by using local definitions to represent shared subexpressions:

```
?  double (square (2+2) + 5)
→  m + m   where   m = (square (2+2) + 5)
→  m + m   where   m = n*n + 5;   n = 2+2
→  m + m   where   m = n*n + 5;   n = 4
→  m + m   where   m = 16 + 5
→  m + m   where   m = 21
→  42
```

In many cases, evaluation order makes no difference to the result. A replacement does not change the value of the expression, and the final normal form is a standard representation of the expression's value, and is independent of the evaluation order. However, innermost evaluation sometimes causes subexpressions which contain errors or infinite loops to be evaluated unnecessarily. For example, with the definition of *invertible* given in Section 2.2.2, the first few steps in the evaluation of *invertible 0* are:

```
?   invertible 0
→   0~=0  &  1/0=0
→   False  &  1/0=0
```

If innermost evaluation were used at this stage, the right hand argument *1/0=0* would be evaluated next, causing a program error. With outermost evaluation, the call to *&* is made next, its second argument is not evaluated at all, and the result *False* is returned.

An evaluation strategy is **lazy** if no subexpression containing an error or infinite loop is ever evaluated unnecessarily. This can be achieved using a particular kind of outermost strategy in which subexpressions can be thought of as being evaluated by demand. The need to print the next character of the result expression creates a demand for information about that expression. If the outermost function call cannot be made, this is because there is not enough information known about one of its arguments, and so the demand for information is transferred to that argument. In this way, the demand reaches an outermost replaceable subexpression – one about which more information is definitely needed.

There are many lazy evaluation strategies, all producing exactly the same results, but differing in efficiency. For example, it is often beneficial to use a mixture of outer and inner reductions, with inner reductions being used only when their use does not lead to unnecessary evaluations. In hand evaluation and in the example evaluations in this book, subexpressions may be replaced in any convenient order, and several steps may be shown as a single step to improve the clarity of the presentation.

The advantages of lazy evaluation are most apparent when it comes to list processing. For example, infinite lists can be handled with no extra language features – the expression *[1,3..]!2* for finding the third odd number is evaluated by the sequence of reduction steps:

```
?   [1,3..]!2
→   (1:[3,5..])!2
→   (1:3:[5,7..])!2
```

$\rightarrow$   $(1:3:5:\underline{[7,9..]}\,!2$
$\rightarrow$   5

When list expressions are evaluated, the normal form of a list is regarded as the form built up from the constructors [] and :. This is despite the fact that Miranda prints lists out in the most convenient form – as raw characters if the result is a list of characters, as string constants for embedded lists of characters, and with square brackets and commas for other lists.

It is only very recently that optimising compilers have been designed which allow programs in lazy languages to run with acceptable efficiency, and much research is still being done. In particular, in a pure language with no side effects, it is difficult to implement data structures such as arrays which are updated in place. For example, suppose there were a function *update xs n x* which updated an array *xs* by replacing its *n*th member with *x*. When this update has been carried out, there is nothing to stop a programmer from accessing both the new array and the old one *xs* at the same time. On the face of it, it seems that such an update function would have to be implemented by making a copy of *xs* on which to perform the update.

For this reason, arrays are often omitted from pure functional languages and, in particular, they are not available in the version of Miranda on which this book is based. Some hybrid languages have features involving side effects which allow data structures to be updated in place. However, acceptably efficient implementations of arrays in pure functional languages are possible without copying, and research is currently being carried out into optimisation techniques which make array access as efficient as in procedural languages. The provision of array facilities in a Miranda module is discussed in Section 4.7, and the possibility of implementing arrays efficiently in functional languages is explored in Section 6.5.3.

## 2.6.2   Input and Output

Lazy evaluation allows interactive input and output to be implemented in pure functional languages. Other declarative languages, i.e. logic programming languages and hybrid functional languages, use language features involving side effects to perform input and output. This spoils their pure nature, making it difficult to predict or prove properties of the interactive behaviour of programs.

Input and output will be covered in detail in Chapter 5, but the information given here covers most simple programs. As we have already mentioned, output is achieved simply by evaluating expressions. An arbitrary stream of characters can be output by evaluating a suitable list of characters.

For input from the keyboard, Miranda provides the standard symbol $- which stands for the list of characters typed at the keyboard while an expression is being evaluated. Most simple programs use line interaction, i.e. they process the input a line at a time. The operating system processes each line before it is passed to the program, so allowing the line to be edited with a DELETE or BACKSPACE key as it is typed. There is also a function *read* which takes a file name and returns the contents of the file as a list of characters.

A standard function *lines* is provided which splits a list of characters into a list of lines according to the newline characters found in it. The standard function *lay* acts as an inverse to this by taking a list of lines and joining them back into a stream of characters containing newlines. Simple interactive programs can be written just by processing a list of lines as you would any other list. For example, a program which reverses each line that is typed in at the keyboard can be implemented by evaluating the expression *lay (map reverse (lines $-))*:

```
?  lay (map reverse (lines $-))
One
enO
Two
owT
...                              (this continues indefinitely)
```

This evaluation continues until you interrupt it, or until you use the end-of-input convention provided on your computer to terminate keyboard input (often CONTROL-D or CONTROL-Z).

This works because, with lazy evaluation, delaying the evaluation of the characters in $- corresponds to delaying the input of characters from the terminal. The evaluation above proceeds roughly as follows. We use the symbol $- to represent the list of characters remaining to be typed in at any stage:

```
?  lay (map reverse (lines $-))
→  lay (map reverse (lines ("One\n" ++ $-)))
→  lay (map reverse ("One" : lines $-)))
→  lay (reverse "One" : map reverse (lines $-))
→  lay ("enO" : map reverse (lines $-))
→  "enO\n" ++ lay (map reverse (lines $-)))
```

```
    output the four characters "enO\n"
    → lay (map reverse (lines $-)))
    ...
```

The first step involves reading the four characters *"One\n"* from the keyboard. In the last step shown, the characters *"enO\n"* are printed, leaving an expression equivalent to the original one representing the processing of the remaining lines.

## 2.7   Style

Although programming style is largely a matter of personal taste, it is important to develop a consistent and logical style, so as to be able to write correct, readable programs with as few problems as possible. In this section, we suggest a few simple style conventions, and explain the reasons for the style chosen for the examples in this book.

The name of a function should be a word such as *sort* or *reverse* which gives the reader an immediate intuitive understanding of the value it stands for, avoiding obscure abbreviations or unnecessary jargon. On the other hand, a formal parameter usually stands for an arbitrary value of some type, and so a short name of only one or two letters is appropriate. In this book, we try to use names which strongly suggest the types of the parameters, reducing the need for type specifications. For example, we use $n$ for numbers, $c$ for characters, $x$ for a parameter of arbitrary type and so on. We also use names ending in $s$ for lists – $ns$ for lists of numbers, $cs$ for lists of characters, $xs$ for lists of arbitrary type. When splitting up a list such as $xs$, we usually use the name $x$ for the head and $rxs$ (remainder of $xs$) for the tail.

Layout is important in Miranda, not just for readability, but also because there is a layout rule designed to reduce the need for semicolons. As with many other programming languages, it is possible to write a complete script on one line with a semicolon at the end of each equation. The layout rule, called the **offside** rule, is that an equation is terminated, without the need for a semicolon, by any text appearing to the left of the first character of its right hand side. For example, the following definition is wrong because an implicit semicolon is placed at the end of the first line:

```
    number  =  1 + 2 + 3 +
        4 + 5 + 6 + 7 + 8        (this example fails)
```

The definition would work if the second line were indented as far as the *1*.

In this book we use a uniform indenting convention which avoids most of the problems which can arise from the offside rule. If an equation has to be continued on a second line, whether it is because it has a long right hand side, or because it uses guards, or because it has local definitions, then it is broken before the = sign, and the whole right hand side indented by a fixed amount. With this convention, the above definition might become:

```
number
=   1 + 2 + 3 + 4 + 5 +
    6 + 7 + 8
```

The use of spaces can also be important. It is often convenient not to put any space round an operator, e.g. *x:ys*, to make expressions more compact. However, it is bad practice to do this when one of the arguments contains a function application. For example, *f x:ys* looks like *f (x:ys)*, whereas it actually means *(f x):ys* since function application binds tighter than any operator. Such expressions should be written either with parentheses or with extra spaces, e.g. *f x : ys*, so that there is less visual ambiguity.

The = sign is used with two different meanings in Miranda. It is both the equation symbol, and also an operator for testing whether values are equal. For example, it is used in both ways in the definition:

```
empty xs   =   xs = []
```

In this book, two spaces have been put on either side of = when used as an equation symbol, to indicate that it binds very loosely – when used as an operator, it binds much more tightly.

When using pattern matching to define a function using several equations, it is good practice to write **disjoint** equations, i.e. ones in which the patterns do not overlap, so that the actual arguments in a call cannot match more than one equation. The equations can then, in principle, be written in any order, which has considerable benefits when doing program transformation or proof. A common exception to this convention is when the last equation is a default one which catches all the remaining cases.

Finally, scripts should include explanatory comments. Comments begin with two vertical bars *||* and continue to the end of the line. Comments have not been used in the examples in this book, because the surrounding text usually supplies the necessary explanation.

## 2.8   Exercises

1. What is wrong with each of the following expressions, assuming that
   they are intended to be evaluated directly without a supporting script?
   In each case, what do you think was intended, and what result would
   the corrected expressions produce?

   ```
   10 / 7 div 3      [2+3]*4    code x        letter "x"
   (1,2)++(3,4)      #'abcd'    max2(1,2)     tl 1:[2..5]
   ```

2. Copy the definition of the function *roots* given in this chapter into
   a script. Use it find the roots of the quadratic *2\*x^2 - 11\*x + 12*.
   Check that the two numbers found really are roots by evaluating the
   quadratic for each to see if it comes out zero.

3. Use the standard function *hd* and a list comprehension with one generator and one filter to find the first power of *2* which is greater than
   a million.

4. Copy the definitions of the types *person* and *sex* and the function
   *name* given in this chapter into a script. Add a definition of a list
   *people* containing a few *person* structures with distinct names to
   act as a database. Define a function *find* which takes a list of people
   and a name and finds the person with that name in the list, using a
   list comprehension. Try out the *find* function using your *people*
   database.

5. Use a list comprehension with two generators and one filter to produce the list *[(1,1), (1,2), ... (5,5)]* of the *15* pairs of integers
   between *1* and *5* for which the first number is less than or equal to
   the second. Find a second list comprehension with just two generators
   and no filter which produces the same list.

6. Use a guarded equation to define a function *sign* which takes a number and returns *-1, 0* or *1* according to whether the number is negative, zero or positive.

7. Use pattern matching to define a function *test* which takes a boolean
   *b* and two values *x* and *y*, and returns *x* if *b* is *True*, and *y* if *b* is
   *False*. What type does the *test* function have, and what does it
   tell you about the possible types which its arguments can have?

8. Define a function *compose3* which composes three functions in the same way that the *compose* function in Section 2.4.4 composes two functions.

9. Create a data file with an editor and then, from within the Miranda system, evaluate an expression using the standard functions *read*, *lines*, *reverse* and *lay* which displays the lines of the data file in reverse order (i.e. the last line, then the second-last line, and so on).

10. Using the standard function *iterate*, define a function *sequence* which takes a number *n* and returns the infinite sequence *[n, n^n, n^(n^n), n^(n^(n^n)), ...]* in which each member after the first is formed from the previous one by applying the function *(n^)*. The sequence clearly converges when *n=1* and diverges to infinity when *n=2*, forming the rapidly increasing sequence *[2, 4, 16, 65536, ...]*. Define a function *lim* which takes a number *n* and finds the limit of the above sequence (the standard function *limit* may work well enough for this purpose). Find, to three decimal places, the largest number between *1* and *2* for which the sequence converges by trial and error.

# Chapter 3

# The Design of Functions

Function definitions are the nuts and bolts of functional programming. They are the smallest components used in constructing programs, and are typically only a few lines long. This chapter introduces the techniques which functional programmers use to design and write such function definitions. One of the advantages of functional programming is that short function definitions provide modularity on a very small scale. Functions are small units which can be designed and tested completely independently before being combined, and yet they can be remarkably powerful.

Designing programs in functional languages is very different from designing programs in procedural languages, and requires different ways of thinking. It is easy enough to understand example programs written by someone else but, as with all styles of programming, it takes time to pick up the functional approach to problem solving, and so gain confidence in designing your own programs. This chapter, as well as providing detailed examples of function definitions, also describes ways of thinking about problems and algorithms from a functional point of view, and develops the design ideas and techniques which functional programmers use in writing function definitions.

Three main approaches to the design of functions are described. In the toolkit approach, you try to solve a problem by using a collection of generally useful problem solving tools. In the recursive approach, you try to break a problem down into smaller but similar subproblems – this often involves looking for a solution in which some kind of processing is repeated, as with the familiar loop constructs in procedural languages. In the transformation approach, you begin with a function definition which clearly represents a solution to the problem but which is impractical, then transform it into a practical definition.

41

## 3.1   The Toolkit Approach

The idea behind this approach is to build up a collection of problem solving techniques – a kit of tools. For any given problem, you look through your kit to see which tools can be adapted or combined to give a solution. Many common tools are provided in the standard constructions and functions of the language, but you can also develop your own tools.

Some of the advantages of the toolkit approach to function design are that definitions can be made short and clear, that particular styles and techniques of programming can be made easy to use, that re-use of software can be encouraged, and that transformation and proof of programs can be made relatively easy.

Many of the tools described in this section are concerned with list processing. Lists are used in many situations in which data structures such as arrays or linked-lists would be used in a procedural language. However, as there is no assignment or any notion of the passage of time in functional languages, lists are also used in many situations where a single variable with a succession of values would be used in a procedural language.

The problem solving techniques which we will describe are mapping, in which each member of a list is processed in the same way in turn; filtering, in which some members of a list are selected to form a sublist; folding, in which the members of a list are combined into a single value; zipping, in which corresponding members from two lists are combined; and iteration, in which an initial value is processed repeatedly to form a sequence of values. The problem of constructing a random number generator is then discussed to illustrate the way in which tools can be selected and combined in solving a given problem.

### 3.1.1   Mapping

How do you produce a list of the powers of two? One way is to regard it as a loop in which you run through the list of numbers $[0, 1, 2, \ldots]$, and for each number $n$ you form the number $2\text{^}n$. This can be pictured as:

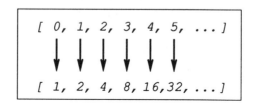

The process of running through a list and doing the same thing to each member to form a new list is called **mapping**. There are two ways in which mapping can be carried out. One is to use the standard list comprehension construct, and the other is to use the standard *map* function. For the powers of two, this leads to the following two equivalent definitions:

```
powers_of_two  =  [2^n | n <- [0..]]
powers_of_two' =  map (2^) [0..]
```

The first of these definitions can be read "the powers of two are the numbers *2^n* where *n* runs through the numbers from *0* upwards", and the second can be read "the powers of two are formed by applying the function *(2^)* to each member of the list *[0..]* ". The form using list comprehension is more flexible, and is usually the better one to use, but it is sometimes clearer to use the *map* function.

As another example, suppose we want to turn a list of words into a title by capitalising each word so that, for example, the list of words *["the", "design", "of", "functions"]* becomes *["The", "Design", "Of", "Functions"]* . Assuming that there is a function available called *capitalise* (see the exercises) which converts the first character of a word to upper case, a function *title* can be written:

```
title ws  =  [capitalise w | w <- ws]
```

which expresses the fact that each word in the given list is to be capitalised in turn.

## 3.1.2   Filtering

How do you define the list of prime numbers? You can do it by running through the list of numbers from *2* upwards and keeping only those whose divisors are just *1* and themselves:

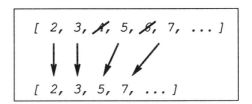

The process of running through a list and keeping only those which pass some test to form a new list is called **filtering**. If we assume that there is a function *divisors* available which returns the list of divisors of a number in ascending order (see the exercises), the list of prime numbers can be defined by filtering using either list comprehension or the standard *filter* function, with either of the two equivalent definitions:

```
primes   =   [n | n <- [2..]; divisors n = [1,n]]


primes'
=   filter prime [2..]   where
    prime n   =   divisors n = [1,n]
```

The first version can be read "the primes are the numbers *n* from *2* upwards for which the divisors of *n* are *1* and *n*". In the second version, there is no simple partially applied function or operator which can be passed as the first argument to filter, so a local function definition is used. The definition can be read "the primes are found by running through *[2..]* picking out the ones which are prime, where *n* is prime if it has divisors *1* and *n*".

As with mapping, the form using list comprehension is more flexible, but it is sometimes clearer to use the *filter* function. Neither of these definitions is very efficient – a more efficient definition of the prime numbers using the sieve method is described in Section 3.2.2.

Part of the power of the list comprehension notation is that mapping and filtering can be combined in a single expression. For example, suppose you want a function which picks out the names of the adults from a list of people, i.e. a list of structures of type *person* as defined in Chapter 2. You could do it with the following function:

```
adults ps   =   [name p | p <- ps; age p >= 18]
```

The function filters the list *ps* to extract those with age at least *18*, and then uses mapping to find the name of each person.

### 3.1.3   Folding

How do you form the sum of a list of numbers? If the standard *sum* function were not available, you could define it yourself as follows. The idea is to put the operator *+* between each pair of members, and evaluate the resulting expression:

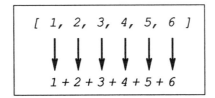

The process of putting an operator between each pair of members of a list and collapsing the result into a single value is called **folding**. The two standard functions `foldl` and `foldr` support folding, one working left to right, and the other right to left. We will use `foldl` for now, and return to the question of when to use `foldr` later.

The `foldl` function takes three arguments. The first is the operator to fold with, the second is the result to be given in the case of the empty list, and the third is the list to be folded. The standard *sum* function is defined by:

```
sum ns  =  foldl (+) 0 ns
```

This specifies that *sum []* is *0* and that, for example, *sum [a,b,c,d]* is *((a+b)+c)+d*. Similarly, the standard function *product* is defined by:

```
product ns  =  foldl (*) 1 ns
```

There is a second way of thinking about folding which is often helpful. You can think of folding with `foldl` as running through the members of a list in order, accumulating a "running total". This running total is initialised to the second argument of `foldl`, and is updated using the function passed as the first argument. For example, in the case of *sum*, the running total is initialised to zero, and has each member of the list added into it in turn.

The standard function *max*, which finds the maximum member of a list, can be defined using `foldl` with a running maximum. The maximum is initialised to the first member of the list and is updated using *max2*:

```
max []      =  error "max of empty list"
max (x:rxs)  =  foldl max2 x rxs
```

In situations like this in which there is no result required for the empty list, or there is no suitable constant which can be used as an initial value (it would have to be $-\infty$ for *max*), a variant `foldl1` of `foldl` which has only two arguments is provided as a standard function. Using `foldl1`, an alternative definition of the *max* function is:

```
    max xs   =   foldl1 max2 xs
```

As another example of the use of *foldl*, a function *count* which counts
the number of occurrences of a value *y* in a list *xs* can be defined by:

```
    count y xs
    =  foldl check 0 xs  where
       check n x
       =  n+1,  if x=y
       =  n,    otherwise
```

This illustrates the fact that the accumulated result need not have the same
type as the members of the list being processed. The local function *check*
takes the current total and the next member of the list, and combines them
to form the new total.

It often makes no difference to the result which of the two functions
*foldl* and *foldr* you use. For example, *foldl (+) 0 [a,b,c,d]* is
equivalent to *((a+b)+c)+d*, whereas *foldr (+) 0 [a,b,c,d]* is equivalent to *a+(b+(c+d))*. However, the *foldl* function is implemented in
such a way that the amount of space used does not grow with the length
of the list being processed in cases like the ones above. For example, the
evaluation of *sum [1..100]* proceeds roughly as follows:

```
    ?   sum [1..100]
    →  foldl (+) 0 [1..100]
    →  foldl (+) 0 (1:[2..100])
    →  foldl (+) (0+1) [2..100]
    →  foldl (+) 1 [2..100]
    ...
```

The amount of space used during an evaluation is essentially the maximum
size of any intermediate expression produced. In this case, laziness ensures
that the list in the third argument is only expanded as needed. The overall
expression does not grow in size as evaluation proceeds. To accomplish this,
*foldl* is given a special implementation in which the second argument
is evaluated at each stage, to avoid it growing into a large unevaluated
expression.

The function *foldr* is, generally speaking, more suitable than *foldl*
in stream processing applications (see Section 3.2.2), despite the fact that
it may take more space. For example, the standard function *and*, which
checks whether every member of a list of booleans is *True*, is defined by:

```
and bs  =  foldr (&) True bs
```

The expression *and [a,b,c,d]* is equivalent to *a& (b& (c&d))*, for example. Since the operator *&* returns *False* when its first argument is *False*, without evaluating its second argument, the effect of using *foldr* is to allow processing to stop as soon as a *False* member is found, whereas *foldl* would continue processing to the end of the list.

Another example of the use of *foldr* is in the definition of the standard function *concat* which joins together a collection of lists into a single list by inserting the *++* operator between them. For example, the list *["abc","def","ghi"]* becomes *"abc"++"def"++"ghi"* which evaluates to *"abcdefghi"*. The *concat* function is defined by:

```
concat xss  =  foldr (++) [] xss
```

In this case, the use of *foldr* allows members of the result list to be returned before *xss* is completely evaluated (see the exercises). In this case, using *foldr* is also more efficient than using *foldl*, because, as mentioned in Section 2.3.1, the time taken by the *++* operator is proportional to the length of its first argument. If *foldl* were used, an expression such as *concat [a,b,c,d]* would become *((a++b)++c)++d*, in which the occurrences of *++* have longer and longer first arguments. Using *foldr*, the expression becomes *a++(b++(c++d))*, in which the first argument of each *++* is a single member of the original list.

As with *foldl*, there is a standard variant *foldr1* of the *foldr* function with one less argument which works on non-empty lists.

### 3.1.4 Zipping

How do you produce a listing of a file with line numbers? Suppose that the file is represented as a list of lines, say *[a,b,c,d,e,f,...]*. The first stage in solving the problem is to pair up each line with its corresponding line number. This can be done by running through the list of line numbers and the list of lines simultaneously, forming a single list of pairs, as shown:

```
                                    6   7, 8, 9, ... ]
                             5
[ (1,a), (2,b), (3,c),   4   d   e   f   g, h, i, ... ]
```

The process of running simultaneously through two lists and forming a single list of pairs is called **zipping**. The standard function *zip2* does exactly that. If the lists are of unequal length, then the excess members of the longer list are discarded. In the line numbering example, a function *list* which takes a list of lines and returns a list of numbered lines can be written:

```
list ls  =   [number n l | (n,l) <- zip2 [1..] ls]
number n l  =   rjustify 4 (shownum n) ++ " " ++ l
```

The two lists *[1..]* and *ls* are zipped together, and then each pair is converted into a numbered line using the *number* function which puts the number in the first four columns, followed by a space, followed by the original line.

The *zip2* function is useful in any context where you want to scan through two lists simultaneously, and process corresponding pairs of members. Miranda provides standard functions *zip3*, *zip4*, ...for scanning several lists simultaneously, forming larger tuples – see Appendix B.

### 3.1.5   Iteration

How do you produce a list of the powers of two? The method described in Section 3.1.1 used the mapping technique. However, when the powers of two are needed in sequence, an alternative method of generating them is to produce each one from the previous one by doubling:

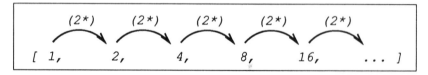

The process of applying a function (the doubling function *(2\*)* in this case) repeatedly to an initial value to produce a sequence of values is called **iteration**. The standard function *iterate* takes a function and an initial value as arguments and returns the constructed list of values. The powers of two can be defined by:

```
powers_of_two  =   iterate (2*) 1
```

The *iterate* function produces an infinite list. There are various ways in which you can extract information from such a list, using list processing functions. For example, you can use *take* or *takewhile* to extract the first few members of the list – lazy evaluation ensures that the remainder of the list is not evaluated.

One common use of iteration is to find a value by successive approximation. The function which is iterated is one which takes an approximation and produces a better one. For example, the standard function *sqrt* which finds the square root of a number can be defined by:

```
sqrt n
=   limit (iterate improve n)   where
      improve r  =  (r + n/r) / 2
```

The local function *improve* takes an approximation *r* to the square root and returns a better approximation (it is a well-known one based on the Newton-Raphson approximation technique). The square root is found by iterating this function on the initial approximation *n*, and then using the standard function *limit* to find the limit of the resulting infinite list of approximations.

The *limit* function is rather too crude for general use in numerical applications. It assumes that the limit has been reached only when it finds two successive members of the list which are exactly equal. It only works because floating point numbers are held to a fixed precision, and even so is very likely to fail because of rounding errors – e.g. if the list ends up oscillating between two very close approximations.

Another standard function *until* is provided to deal with iteration towards a limit in a more general way. Its first argument is a function used to test each value in turn to see if it is good enough to return as the result, and it has two further arguments which are the same as those of *iterate*. It generates the values in turn, and returns the first one which passes the test. Thus a better definition of *sqrt* might be one which stops when the approximation is correct to (say) twelve significant figures:

```
sqrt n
=   until near improve n   where
      near r  =  abs (1 - n/r^2) < 1e-12
      improve r  =  (r + n/r) / 2
```

The *until* function can be used in any circumstance where you want to generate a sequence of values by iteration until you find one satisfying some criterion. For example, to find the first power of two larger than a million you can write:

```
first_big_power_of_two  =  until (>10^6) (2*) 1
```

### 3.1.6   Random Numbers

How do you implement a random number generator in a functional language? Answering this question will allow us to use some of the tools we have been looking at in a slightly more realistic example.

In procedural languages, random numbers are often implemented using a procedure which returns a different number each time it is called. In functional languages, this cannot be done. Instead, the (potentially infinite) stream of numbers which such a procedure would return is defined directly as a list. This is similar to the way in which keyboard input is represented as a list of characters $- rather than a procedure which returns a character each time it is called – see the discussion of stream functions in Section 3.2.2. One very common kind of (pseudo) random number generator is based on an integer function such as:

```
randomise n  =   (n*b+1) mod m
m  =  10^8
b  =  31415821
```

This function takes one random number and produces the next. The constants *m* and *b* have to be chosen carefully, as described in the book by Sedgewick [13], in order to ensure randomness. Miranda has no limit on the size of integers, so there are no overflow problems in computing *n*b+1*. A list of random numbers can be generated using iteration, starting with some suitable initial value:

```
iterate randomise 1234567
```

Only the first *5* or *6* digits of the numbers generated can be treated as "random" because the rightmost digits oscillate. Also, the numbers are between *0* and *10^8-1*, which is not a very convenient range. A common approach which solves both these problems is to scale the numbers down so that they become floating point numbers between *0* and *1*. The mapping technique can be used for this. The complete definition of the list of random floating point numbers can then be written:

```
random_reals
=  [n/10^8 | n <- iterate randomise 1234567]
   where
   randomise n = (n*b+1) mod m
   m  =  10^8
   b  =  31415821
```

If random integers in some range *0* to *n-1* are required, the floating point numbers in the list *random_reals* can be multiplied up by *n* and the integer part taken using the standard *entier* function. This will work well with values of *n* up to about *10^5* or *10^6*. Again, the mapping technique can be used:

```
random_integers n
=  [entier (r*n) | r<-random_reals]
```

If several different random sequences are required for some application, then the sequences above can be adjusted, for example by using the standard *drop* function to remove some numbers from the beginning, or else by providing versions of the above definitions with an extra argument to allow the initial value (the "seed") to be specified.

## 3.2 The Recursion Approach

The idea behind recursion is to break a problem down into smaller subproblems of the same kind. The solutions to the subproblems are then combined into a solution to the main problem. A **recursive** function definition is one based on this approach. Such a function calls itself with simpler argument values to solve the subproblems.

Recursion is one of the main ways in which the flow of control is defined in functional languages. In particular, it replaces the loop constructs of procedural languages. It can be used to design functions for which existing tools are inadequate, or to define new tools. In particular, recursion is used to implement most of the tools described in the previous section. Because recursion plays such a prominent part in functional programming, it is important to think about it from as many different angles as possible.

In this section, we will look first at loops. These form a special case of recursion in which values are repeatedly simplified until a direct result can be given. Next, we look at stream functions which process lists incrementally, generating members of their result lists at the same time as processing members of their argument lists. Finally we will discuss direct ways of thinking about recursion in its full generality.

### 3.2.1  Loops

A recursive **loop** is a particularly simple kind of recursive definition, sometimes called a **tail-recursive** definition, in which a problem is reduced to a simpler problem of the same kind. A loop function calls itself with simpler arguments which represent a situation which is closer to the solution than before. One of the main advantages of recursive loops over procedural ones is that they are self-contained, and so can easily be generalised and re-used.

A loop can be designed by looking for a solution in which some kind of processing is repeated. Once you have the idea for an algorithm of this kind, the next task is to determine the essential values which change each time round the loop. These become the arguments to a recursive loop function. Once you have determined the way in which the arguments change, and what the termination conditions are, you are in a position to write down the function's definition.

To illustrate this design process, we will look at three example problems for which loop design produces a good solution – finding the length of a list, reversing a list, and line editing.

How do you find the length of a list? There is a standard operator # for doing this, but how do you write your own *length* function to do the same job? One solution is to design a loop in which you run along the list and count the members. The loop function has two arguments, one representing a running total of the number of members seen so far, and the other representing the current position in the list. In a procedural loop, you might keep track of the current position using an index or pointer into the original list. However, the members counted already are of no further interest, and so it is only necessary to keep track of the list of remaining members. Having determined these two loop arguments, their successive values in finding the length of, say, *[a, b, c, d]* can be pictured as follows:

| running total | remaining list |
|:---:|:---:|
| *0* | *[a, b, c, d]* |
| *1* | *[b, c, d]* |
| *2* | *[c, d]* |
| *3* | *[d]* |
| *4* | *[]* |

The loop terminates when the second argument becomes empty. In the general case, the first argument changes by being incremented, and the second by having its first member removed. The loop can be written as a function *count* with two arguments, defined by two equations using pattern matching:

```
count n []    =   n
count n (x:rxs)   =   count (n+1) rxs
```

The first equation deals with the termination case (second argument empty), returning the final value of the running total. The second equation deals with the general case (second argument non-empty), and specifies that the loop is re-entered with two new values for its arguments. The name *count* can be thought of as a name for the loop, and the right hand side of the second equation can be read "go round the loop again with the running total set to *n+1* and the remaining members set to *rxs*".

If you simulate the evaluation of *count 0 [a,b,c,d]* using the method described at the end of the last chapter, you will see that it progresses exactly as in the above picture. The *length* function can finally be defined:

```
length xs
=   count 0 xs  where
    count n []    =  n
    count n (x:rxs)  =   count (n+1) rxs
```

The *length* function initialises the loop by calling *count* with zero as the first argument. The *count* function has been given a local definition, assuming that it is not going to be needed for any other purpose.

It is also possible to define the *length* function using tools, e.g. by mapping and summing (see the exercises). Which method you choose depends on efficiency, programming style, and so on.

As a second example of loop design, how do you reverse a list, i.e. how do you define the standard *reverse* function? In a procedural language, you might consider reversing an array (say) in place, but that is not a suitable algorithm for a general purpose procedure, since the original array might still be wanted. In any case, there is no notion of updating in place in most functional languages. Thus it is best to use an algorithm in which, at each stage, a member is taken from the original list and added to a new, reversed list.

The two arguments of the loop function are the remainder of the original list which has yet to be dealt with, and the part of the result list which has been constructed so far. The steps involved in reversing the list *[1,2,3,4,5]* can be pictured as follows:

| remaining list | reversed list |
|---|---|
| *[1,2,3,4,5]* | *[]* |
| *[2,3,4,5]* | *[1]* |
| *[3,4,5]* | *[2,1]* |
| *[4,5]* | *[3,2,1]* |
| *[5]* | *[4,3,2,1]* |
| *[]* | *[5,4,3,2,1]* |

The loop terminates when the first list is empty, and in the general case, one member is moved from the front of the first list to the front of the second. A loop function *move* which captures this algorithm can be defined:

```
move [] ys  =  ys
move (x:rxs) ys  =  move rxs (x:ys)
```

To define the *reverse* function itself, the definition of *move* can be made local, and called with *[]* as its second argument:

```
reverse xs
=  move xs []  where
   move [] ys  =  ys
   move (x:rxs) ys  =  move rxs (x:ys)
```

This definition only involves access to the front of lists, so this is a reasonably efficient version of the *reverse* function. It is also possible to define *reverse* without recursion by folding with *foldl*, as in Appendix B, and indeed this may provide a more efficient implementation if the standard function *foldl* itself has a built-in, optimised implementation.

A third problem which benefits from being tackled using recursive loop design is the problem of line editing. When a program uses line interaction (see Chapter 5), the operating system normally allows each line to be edited before it is passed to the program. A 'delete' or 'backspace' key can be used to delete the last character typed. If a program uses character interaction, so that each character is passed directly to the program, the program may have to perform this processing itself in some circumstances. A simplified version of the problem is this. Given a string in which a 'delete' character, say *'X'*, indicates deletion of the previous character, convert this into the intended string. For example, the string:

```
"I anXm nitXXot very good at tyingXXXping."
```

is to be processed into the intended string:

```
"I am not very good at typing."
```

The natural algorithm to solve this is to scan forwards through the characters in the string, simulating the effect of the X characters. This can be thought of as a loop function with two arguments. The first is the list of characters already processed, and the second is the list of characters remaining to be processed. It is useful to picture a few steps in the algorithm to get a feel for what happens:

```
....                                            ....
"I am ni"     "tXXot very good at tyingXXXping."
"I am nit"    "XXot very good at tyingXXXping."
"I am ni"     "Xot very good at tyingXXXping."
"I am n"      "ot very good at tyingXXXping."
"I am no"     "t very good at tyingXXXping."
....                                            ....
```

At each stage, one character is taken from the front of the second string, and one character is added to or taken from the end of the first string. To deal with all the cases properly, we have to decide what happens if a delete character appears when the first string is empty. The usual convention is just to discard it. A loop function *step* can be written:

```
step xs []   =   xs
step xs (y:rys)
=   step (xs++[y]) rys,   if y ~= del
=   step (init xs) rys,   if xs ~= []
=   step xs rys,          otherwise
del   =   'X'
```

The first equation deals with termination of the loop, which is when the second string is empty. The second equation uses guards to define three cases – when a normal character is processed, when a deletion character is processed, and when a deletion character appears with the first string empty. The final equation defines the deletion character.

The main operations on the first list are *xs++[y]* and *init xs* which are inefficient since they involve scanning the list *xs*. It would be more efficient to store *xs* in the reverse order during processing, so that the operations involve only the front of the list.

If we make this change to the way *xs* is stored, remove the definition of *del*, and make the definition of *step* local to a function *edit* which takes the original line and *del* as arguments, the result is:

```
edit line del
=   step [] line where
    step xs []   =   reverse xs
    step xs (y:rys)
    =   step (y:xs) rys,   if y ~= del
    =   step (tl xs) rys,  if xs ~= []
    =   step [] rys,       otherwise
```

This definition can now be used in a variety of situations, and indeed is not restricted to strings. The argument `line` can be a list of values of any type, provided that `del` is a value of that same type.

### 3.2.2   Stream Functions

One serious limitation of recursive loops, as described above, is that they do not return any results until they terminate. In list processing applications, functions often need to return result lists member by member as they go along.

A **stream** is a list which is thought of as having its members produced one by one as required – for instance, a list of characters typed on the keyboard during the running of an interactive program, or an infinite list which 'unwinds' as needed.

In procedural languages, a stream is usually implemented as a procedure which returns one item from the stream each time it is called – e.g. a procedure which reads a character from the keyboard, or a procedure which generates a new random number each time it is called. Pure functional languages like Miranda do not need separate types or notations for streams because all lists are treated as streams.

A **stream function** is a function which takes one stream as its input and produces another as its output. For example, it might take a stream of characters and chop it up into a stream of words, or it might perform some processing on the members of an infinite list. A stream function must output members of its result list at the same time as it inputs members of its argument list, so that the streams "flow" with as little intermediate storage or delay as possible.

As an example of the problem, take the standard function `map` which applies a given function `f` to each member of a list to form a new list. Following the loop design ideas above, `map` could be defined using a loop function of two arguments:

```
map f xs
= maploop [] xs  where
  maploop ys []   = ys
  maploop ys (x:rxs)  =  maploop (ys ++ [f x]) rxs
```

However, with this definition, `map` does not return any results until the entire input list is evaluated. This means that it cannot be used in interactive situations, or with infinite lists. Moreover, when it can be used, it takes up much more space than necessary in storing the evaluated input list and the processed output list. Such unnecessary use of space is sometimes called a **space leak.**

The direct loop design approach may be appropriate when it is clear that a list processing function cannot return any result until it has scanned the whole of its argument list, as can be verified for the example functions *length, reverse* and *edit* given earlier, but it is not appropriate for stream functions.

In many cases, stream functions can be designed by a slight variant on loop design in which accumulators are avoided. An **accumulator** is a loop argument which merely gathers up the members of the result list, as with *ys* in the above definition. This argument can be omitted, and the loop function can be made to return the first member of the result before going back round the loop. The definition of *map* becomes:

```
map f xs
=  maploop xs  where
   maploop []  =  []
   maploop (x:rxs)  =  f x : maploop rxs
```

The first equation for *maploop* says that when the input list is empty, there are no more members of the output list to be produced. The second equation says that for a non empty input list, the first member of the result is *f x*, and the remaining members are produced by going back round the loop to process the tail of the argument list.

In fact, the definition can be simplified further by adding *f* as an extra loop argument, despite the fact that it does not change each time round the loop, because then *map* can be treated as its own loop function:

```
map f []  =  []
map f (x:rxs)  =  f x : map f rxs
```

We can check that, with this definition, *map* can be used as a stream function by following the evaluation of *map (^2) [1..]*, which proceeds as follows, in a way which uses only a small constant amount of space:

```
?  map (^2) [1..]
→  map (^2) (1:[2..])
→  1^2 : map (^2) [2..]
→  1 : map (^2) [2..]
output the number 1
→  map (^2) [2..]
...
```

Most of the standard list processing functions and notations can be used as stream functions in this way, and such functions can be combined into "pipelines" which process streams using a minimum of space.

As another example of a stream function, consider the problem of finding the prime numbers using the sieve method, which is described by Sedgewick [13]. Sieving is a method which is superior to the one described earlier on in the chapter. It is the sort of algorithm which you should not necessarily expect to be able to think up for yourself, but which you should expect to be able to implement in a functional language once you have looked it up and understood it.

The sieve algorithm can most easily be pictured as a loop function with two arguments. The first is the list of prime numbers generated so far – an accumulator. The second is the list of remaining candidates – it includes only numbers which are not divisible by any of the primes generated so far. The first few steps in the determination of the list of primes up to *100* can be pictured as follows. The initial candidate list is the list *[2..100]*:

```
[]          [2,3,4,5,6,7,8,9,10,11,12,13,14,15,...,100]
[2]         [3,5,7,9,11,13,15,17,19,21,23,...,99]
[2,3]       [5,7,11,13,17,19,23,25,29,...,97]
[2,3,5]     [7,11,13,17,19,23,29,...,97]
....        ....
```

At each step the first member of the candidate list is added to the end of the accumulator, and the first candidate and all its multiples are deleted from the candidate list. The loop terminates when the candidate list runs out.

If we avoid the use of an accumulating argument, this algorithm leads to a definition for a function *sieve* which has the candidate list as its only argument. It returns the first member and filters the numbers which are not multiples of it from the remainder:

```
sieve []  =  []
sieve (n:rns)
   =  n : sieve [m | m<-rns; m mod n ~= 0]
```

This definition can be used with infinite lists (in which case the first equation is never used), allowing us to define the infinite list of all primes:

```
primes  =  sieve [2..]
```

The *sieve* function counts as a stream function, because it outputs members of the result list as it goes along. However, the amount of space it uses grows during processing because more and more partially evaluated list expressions are generated as each new prime number found is used to filter the remaining list.

### 3.2.3   General Recursion

The loop design approach to writing function definitions is only one way of thinking about recursion, and it only applies directly to a limited range of problems. It can be indirectly helpful in more general circumstances, however, in trying to determine what arguments a function should have in order to solve a given problem, as we have seen with stream functions.

With more general forms of recursion, the problem is not just to determine what arguments might be needed, but also to determine how solutions to subproblems can be used in constructing an overall solution to a problem.

One general design method which you can adopt is to tackle a problem by assuming that you have a solution to a slightly simpler subproblem, and by finding a way of converting it into a solution to the main problem. For example, to design a definition of a function *fac*, where *fac n* is the factorial of *n*, i.e. the product of the numbers from *1* to *n*, imagine that you have the value of *fac (n-1)* and use this to construct *fac n*. Of course, there must always be a simple case in which a direct result can be given, so as to terminate the recursion. A possible definition for *fac* is:

```
fac n
=  1,              if n=0
=  n * fac (n-1),  otherwise
```

It is also possible to define *fac* without recursion using the standard *product* function – see the exercises.

In general, when writing a recursive definition, you do not need to worry about where the solution to the subproblem comes from – it is as if you give the subproblem to a friend, wait until the friend returns the result, and then process it to solve the main problem.

There are cases where two or more subproblems of a similar kind are solved and their solutions combined to form an overall solution. Algorithms of this kind are called **divide and conquer** algorithms. One example is in the definition of the standard *sort* function, for which the merge sort algorithm can be used (see Sedgewick [13]). The argument list is split in two, the two halves are sorted using two recursive calls, and the result lists merged together with the standard *merge* function:

```
sort xs
=  xs,                                 if #xs<=1
=  merge (sort ys) (sort zs),  otherwise
   where
   ys  =  take half xs
   zs  =  drop half xs
   half  =  #xs div 2
```

Another divide and conquer algorithm for sorting, the quick sort algorithm, is shown in Appendix B. The advantage of these algorithms over simpler ones such as insertion sort with only a single recursive call is that they take a time proportional to $n * log\ n$ rather than $n*n$ on lists of length $n$. Such definitions might also be more appropriate for a parallel computer, since the two recursive calls are independent, and could in principle be evaluated at the same time.

The standard functions listed in Appendix B provide many examples of simple recursive definitions. With practice, such definitions can be written down quickly and directly using the design ideas introduced in this section. In fact, there is often a choice of techniques, and many different definitions are possible for the same function.

## 3.3   The Transformation Approach

The transformation approach to the design of functions is perhaps the most sophisticated of the methods described in this chapter. Program transformation is a powerful unifying theme in functional programming, having strong links with evaluation, compilation, semantics and proofs of program properties. Some of these links will be discussed more fully in later chapters.

The transformation approach is one of the most suitable ones for use in computer-aided support packages which help a programmer to develop programs, looking after "book-keeping" details and helping to ensure the correctness of the final program. There is a considerable amount of research effort being put into developing such support packages at present.

The ideas behind program transformation can also be used rather more informally in developing programs by hand. The general approach is to begin with a **specification** of the task to be performed. This specification may be regarded as an implicit definition of the function which solves the problem, and the aim is to transform it into an explicit definition. Alternatively, an explicit but inefficient definition might be transformed into a more efficient one.

A **transformation** step is carried out on an expression by replacing one subexpression by another equivalent one. Certain stylised forms of transformation, such as evaluation and compilation, are fully automatable. Others, such as program proof and the program design process described here, can only ever be semi-automated and will always have to be guided by human intervention.

There are many situations in which transformation can be useful. We will give one example from each of three general areas in which transformation can be used. The first example is one where a multiple pass algorithm is transformed into a single pass algorithm. The second example is one we have already seen earlier in the chapter – the elimination of an accumulator from a loop function to produce a stream function. The final example involves the development of an inverse to a given function.

## 3.3.1   Reducing the Number of Passes

As a very simple example of a multiple pass algorithm, suppose we have a definition of a function *sumsq* which finds the sum of the squares of a list of numbers:

```
sumsq ns  =  sum (map (^2) ns)
```

This apparently involves two passes through the list *ns*, one to form the squares and the second to sum them. Suppose we decide to find a new recursive definition for *sumsq* which makes only one pass through *ns*, using the old definition as a specification. We assume that the new definition has the form:

```
sumsq []  =  0
sumsq (n:rns)  =  ...
```

We can now use transformation to find the right hand side of the second equation. We will use a similar notation for transformation as we have been using up until now for evaluation. The main difference is that transformation is not an automatic process – we have to choose what to do at each step, and we can replace any subexpression by any equivalent one. The transformation steps might be:

```
 ?  sumsq (n:rns)
 →  sum (map (^2) (n:rns))
 →  sum (n^2 : map (^2) rns)
 →  n^2 + sum (map (^2) rns)
 →  n^2 + sumsq rns
```

The first step uses the original definition, the second and third use properties of *map* and *sum*, and the final step uses the original definition in the reverse direction.

The resulting function may not be more efficient. Two simple passes may be as efficient as one complex one, and laziness ensures that if both passes are stream functions, they will be executed together in step as the argument list is evaluated. However, in more complicated cases, and particularly for algorithms on complex data structures such as trees, transforming a multiple pass algorithm into a single pass one can produce considerable savings.

Although the transformation method has some built-in guarantees of correctness, since it involves replacing one subexpression by another one which has the same value, these guarantees are not absolute. In particular, the equations obtained at the end, although correct, may not be suitable for use as defining equations, or they may not cover all possible cases, so they need to be checked, as the next example illustrates.

## 3.3.2  Eliminating Accumulators

When we were discussing stream functions above, we used the *map* function as an example. The direct loop design method produces a loop function *map'* , say, which we might conveniently define as:

```
map' f ys []      =   ys
map' f ys (x:rxs)   =   map' f (ys ++ [f x]) rxs
```

Our goal is to transform this into the usual definition of *map*, which is suitable for use as a stream function, by eliminating the accumulating argument *ys*. In other words, the specification for the function *map* is:

```
map f xs   =   map' f [] xs
```

We are looking for a direct definition of the *map* function of the form:

```
map f []    =   []
map f (x:rxs)   =   ...
```

The way we do this is to use transformation to find the right hand side of the second equation:

```
?   map f (x:rxs)
→   map' f [] (x:rxs)
→   map' f ([] ++ [f x]) rxs
```

```
  →  map' f [f x] rxs
  →  f x : map' f [] rxs
  →  f x : map f rxs
```

The first and last steps use the specifying equation. The second and third steps use properties of *map'* and the *++* operator. The fourth step is the most interesting one. It uses the fact that the following equation holds for all suitable *f*, *ys* and *xs*:

$$map' \ f \ ys \ xs \ = \ ys \ ++ \ map' \ f \ [] \ xs$$

Strictly speaking, this equation requires proof. It says that *ys* is an accumulator – *ys* accumulates the result list, and the members of *ys* at any stage will not be involved in any further processing, so they can be output, and the loop re-started with the empty list. Given any loop function with an accumulator which satisfies an equation like this, the same transformation process can be carried out to eliminate the accumulator and produce a stream function.

It is worth noting that *map* and *map'* are not identical functions – *map* works in stream processing situations where *map'* does not. In fact, this transformation could have been carried in the reverse direction, obtaining *map'* from *map*. In that case, we would have ended up with a less powerful definition. Transformation cannot be carried out blindly – the result must be checked to see if it is suitable for its intended purpose.

### 3.3.3   Finding Inverses

Another situation in which the transformation approach can be valuable is when designing a function which is, in some sense, an inverse of some other function for which we already have a definition. For example, how do you write a function *unzip2* which unzips a list of pairs into two separate lists? This is an inverse of the function *zip2*, in the sense that we can use the following equation as a specification:

$$unzip2 \ (zip2 \ xs \ ys) \ = \ (xs,ys)$$

This equation only holds when *xs* and *ys* have the same length, but it is sufficient as an implicit definition of *unzip2* because every list of pairs can be regarded as the result of zipping together two lists of equal length. We are looking for an explicit recursive definition of the form:

```
unzip2 []   =   ([],[])
unzip2 ((x,y):rxys)   =   ...
```

The transformation method helps determine the right hand side of the second equation. In this case, it is easier to understand the transformation process if we perform replacements on the specifying equation as a whole. The transformation steps are:

```
?   unzip2 (zip2 xs ys)   =   (xs,ys)
→   unzip2 (zip2 (x:rxs) (y:rys))   =   (x:rxs,y:rys)
→   unzip2 ((x,y) : zip2 rxs rys)   =   (x:rxs,y:rys)
→   unzip2 ((x,y):rxys)
    =   (x:rxs,y:rys) where (rxs,rys)   =   unzip2 rxys
```

In the first step, $x:rxs$ and $y:rys$ are substituted for $xs$ and $ys$. The second step uses the definition of $zip2$. In the final step, a new parameter $rxys$ is introduced as a name for $zip2$ $rxs$ $rys$, and $rxs$ and $rys$ are expressed in terms of $rxys$ by defining $(rxs,rys)$ to be $unzip2$ $rxys$.

This transformation illustrates the fact that other transformation steps can be applied besides simple replacement of subexpressions. The transformation technique is rather like the process of constructing proofs in mathematics. It involves being familiar with a wide range of properties of the functions you use, and it involves intelligence and skill in guiding the transformation in useful directions.

On the other hand, the individual steps are simple, and usually involve little more than what is called **equational reasoning**, i.e. the ability to use equations to replace subexpressions with equivalent ones. The technique can be very powerful and reliable, particularly with computer support to handle the details. It is perhaps the most difficult design method to carry out by hand, but it does provide an extra measure of confidence in the correctness of definitions.

## 3.4   Exercises

1. Write a non-recursive definition of the factorial function $fac$ using the standard $product$ function.

2. Write a non-recursive definition of the function $length$ using mapping and the standard $sum$ function – map each member of the list to the number $1$ and sum the result.

3. Write a definition of a function *divisors* which returns the list of divisors of a number, using a list comprehension.

4. Write a function *capitalise* which converts the first letter of a lower case word to upper case using the standard functions *code* and *decode*. You do not need to know what codes the letters have, only that the lower case ones have consecutive code numbers, as do the upper case ones.

5. Define a version *cat* of the standard function *concat* using *foldl* rather than *foldr*. Verify that they have the same effect on finite lists by trying out a few examples. Demonstrate that *concat* works on infinite lists and *cat* does not by applying both functions to the list *repeat "abc"*.

6. Define a function *join* which joins two words together with a space in between. Use *join*, *capitalise* and *foldr1* to define a function *sentence* which takes a list of words such as *["the", "cat", "sat", "on", "the", "mat"]* and produces a sentence such as *"The cat sat on the mat."* by joining the words, capitalising the first word, and adding a full stop.

7. Write a definition of a function *average* which finds the average of a list of numbers by designing a recursive loop function *av* with three arguments – a running total, a running count, and the list of remaining members.

8. A **fibonacci** sequence is an infinite list of numbers in which each member from the third one onwards is the sum of the previous two, e.g. *[1,1,2,3,5,8,13,...]*. Define a recursive function *fib* with two arguments $m$ and $n$ which returns the fibonacci sequence beginning with $m$ and $n$.

9. Write a recursive definition of a function *rev* which reverses a list in the same way as the standard function *reverse*. The function *rev* should reverse the tail of its argument list, and then attach the head to the end. This is often called the "naive" definition of the reverse function. Why is *rev* much less efficient than *reverse*?

10. Design definitions for some of the standard functions in Appendix B (giving them different names to avoid name clashes) and then compare your definitions with the originals.

11. Use the transformation approach to design a single pass version of the function:

```
pos ns  =  # (filter (>0) ns)
```

Is the new version more or less efficient than the original?

12. Use Miranda to find the (unique!) solution to the following puzzle. Find a number made up from the digits *1* to *9*, used once each, such that the number formed from the first *n* digits is divisible by *n*, for each *n* from *1* to *9*. Define a recursive function *answers* with one argument *n* which returns the list of all partial answers with *n* digits. It should run through all the partial answers of length *n-1* and, for each one, run through the list of digits not already used, attaching them to the end and testing for divisibility by *n*.

# Chapter 4

# The Design of Modules

Modules are large self-contained components used in program construction. A **module** is a collection of related declarations and definitions, usually gathered together into a single script and compiled as a single unit. Modules are used for two main purposes. One is to split a program into manageable units which can be developed independently. The other is to provide general purpose facilities which can be re-used in several programs – these are often called library modules.

The key feature of modules which makes module design more than just a matter of collecting together a few related definitions is that a module should be capable of being developed and maintained independently of other modules. Changes made to one module while developing it should have as little impact on the rest of the program as possible. This means that the interfaces between modules should be simple and stable, and that the facilities which a module provides should be clearly specified.

The first section in this chapter discusses the interfaces between modules, and the extra language features which Miranda provides for defining and controlling these interfaces. The second section discusses the specification of the facilities provided by a module, and the generality and efficiency issues which arise, particularly for library modules. The remaining sections give examples of important library modules for handling queues, sets, trees, tables, arrays and graphs.

## 4.1   Interfaces

If modules are to be developed independently, then it is important that changes can be made to a module with a minimum of disruption to the rest

of the program. If a module in a large program changes, it is intolerable to
have to check all the calls made to functions in that module to see if they
are still valid.

To achieve this independence of modules, a module must appear smaller
from the outside than it does from the inside. A module **interface** is a description of the functions which are provided by a module and their types.
It forms a cut-down view of the facilities which a module provides which
excludes implementation details and which represents just sufficient information about the module for it to be used correctly in the remainder of a
program.

An interface needs to be simple, so that users of a module can get a clear
picture of what the module does and how to use it, while concentrating on
the programming details of other modules. The interface also needs to be
stable, so that the module can be developed with as little change to the
interface as possible, and thus as little change to the rest of the program as
possible.

Although modules are self-contained logical units of programs, rather
than physical units, it is convenient to put each module into a separate
script, to allow modules to be edited and compiled separately. This section describes the ways in which module interfaces can be controlled using
language features for including one script in another, changing the set of
names which is exported from one script and imported into another, defining parameterised scripts whose facilities depend on functions provided by
the programs which use them, and forming abstract types which are like
data structures in which the representation used is hidden from view.

### 4.1.1   Separate Scripts

A program can be built up from several scripts. The advantages of this
are that it keeps source files down to a manageable size, and that it allows
for separate editing and compilation. When developing a program, only
those scripts which have changed need to be re-compiled. This corresponds
very closely to the need to develop modules independently, so it is usual to
put each module into a separate script, and to use the words "script" and
"module" interchangeably.

Each program consists of a main module which includes all the other
modules which are needed. For example, the following diagram describes
two programs. The first is made up from the three modules *main1*, *sub1*
and *sub2*, and the second from *main2*, *sub2* and *sub3*. The module *sub2*
might be a library module which is provided for general use:

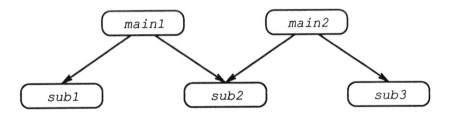

The way in which one module includes another is to use a `%include` declaration. For example, the `main1` module would contain the following two lines:

```
%include "sub1"
%include "sub2"
```

The effect is similar to including the source text of the two modules directly into the main module – all their top level functions and types become available for use.

The inclusions can be quite complicated, with library modules including other library modules and so on, but the pattern of inclusions must not contain any cycles. For example, there cannot be two scripts each of which includes the other.

The pattern of inclusions determines the order of compilation – a script must be compiled before any other script which includes it. The Miranda system takes care of this for you – whenever a script is compiled, the system first checks to make sure that all the scripts which it includes, directly or indirectly, have also been compiled since they were last altered, and compiles them if necessary.

### 4.1.2 Imports and Exports

Module interfaces are not separated out in Miranda. Indeed, a module need not have an explicit interface, in which case the interface implicitly consists of the names of all the functions defined in the module, together with their types. The compiler checks that functions are called with the correct types, even across modules, so the types need not be declared. However, it is good practice to include type declarations in the module to provide compiler-checked documentation of the facilities which the module provides.

Since modules are developed independently, the collection of function names provided by one module may not be suitable for use in another. Miranda provides facilities for changing the set of names, both when exporting them from one module, and when importing them into another.

The %export declaration is used to avoid exporting support functions, i.e. ones which are there merely to help in defining the main functions. The declaration simply gives a list of the names of the functions and types which are to be exported. The default, if no %export declaration is given, is to export all the names defined at the top level in a module, but not the names which the module itself imports from elsewhere.

For example, a module for handling sets as sorted lists without duplicates might contain three functions: *setof* for converting a list into a set, *union* for combining two sets, and *unique* for removing duplicates from a sorted list. The %export declaration can be used to export only *setof* and *union*, but not *unique*:

```
%export setof union

setof xs   =   unique (sort xs)
union xs ys  =   unique (merge xs ys)
unique xs  =   ...
```

The function *unique* is a support function whose definition appears in Section 4.4, as part of a more complete set module. It is defined as a top level function rather than being put in a **where** clause because it is used in both of the other function definitions. The *unique* function only exists because of the particular representation chosen for sets – by not exporting *unique*, programs cannot use it, and we are free to switch to some other representation for sets which does not use *unique* in the future without making existing programs fail.

Another use for the %export declaration is to export functions which have been included from some other script. These are not normally exported because they are usually used as support functions. However, if you are writing a module which is an extension of an existing library module, say, you might want to export all the functions which you import, together with the new functions which you define. As a useful abbreviation, the %export declaration can include the name of an imported module, in double quotes, to represent all the items imported from that module. For example, a module which extended the set module by adding a universal set and a complement operation might have the interface:

```
%include "sets"
%export "sets" universe complement
```

When a module is included, the including module can control the names which it imports. The %include declaration can contain a list of names to be excluded or re-named. One situation which makes this feature vital is when two library modules which have been developed independently contain functions with the same names. For example, suppose there are two modules *sets* and *objects* which both contain *size* and *insert* functions. Then a program might include both modules with the declarations:

```
%include "sets" -size
%include "objects" plug/insert
```

This specifies that the *size* function is not to be imported from the set module (assuming that the program does not need it) so that it does not clash with the *size* function from the object module. The *insert* function from the object module is renamed as *plug* so that it can be used alongside the set *insert* function without a name clash.

### 4.1.3 Parameterised Modules

We have seen that the pattern of module inclusion must not contain cycles. However, there are situations in which mutually recursive modules are desirable. For example, suppose we want to define a library module *order* which provides generalised versions *gmax2*, *gsort*, *gmerge*, ... of the standard functions *max2*, *sort*, *merge*, ... which use some ordering other than the standard one. The generalised functions are to use a function *compare* which compares two values and returns, say, *-1* if the first is less than the second, *0* if they are equal, and *1* otherwise. Any comparison function can be provided, e.g. one which compares people by age.

It would be possible to pass *compare* as an extra argument to each of the generalised functions, but this would be cumbersome as *compare* would have to appear in every call. We want a main program to be able to export its particular *compare* function to the *order* module, and for *order* to export the resulting generalised functions back to the main program.

To allow identifiers such as *compare* to be exported from a main module into a library module, and to allow the library module to be reused in different programs without having to be recompiled, Miranda provides a separate mechanism – **module parameters**. A library module such as *order* is regarded as a parameterised module – the *compare* function is a parameter which need not be the same each time the module is included.

In order to avoid the need for recompilation, the type of the *compare* function must be declared in the *order* module. This is done with the *%free* declaration, which lists the parameters of a module, along with their types. The *order* module might begin with:

```
%free thing::type; compare::thing->thing->num;

gmax2 x y
=   x,   if compare x y >= 0
=   y,   otherwise


    . . .
```

The special keyword **type** is used to declare *thing* as an unknown type,
and then *compare* is declared as a function which takes two *thing*s and
returns a number. This is sufficient to allow the module to be compiled
independently of the programs which use it.

A script which includes the *order* module must explicitly declare what
the type *thing* and the function *compare* are to be replaced by in its
%*include* declaration. The script can then use *gmax2* etc. as required:

```
%include "order" thing==person; compare=older;

older p1 p2
=   -1,   if age p1 < age p2
=    0,   if age p1 = age p2
=    1,   if age p1 > age p2


    . . .
```

It is possible for a script to include *order* twice, providing different
versions of *thing* and *compare* each time, provided that it renames at
least one version of each of the functions *gmax2* etc. so as to avoid name
clashes.

### 4.1.4   Abstract Types

A module can very often be thought of as defining a new type. For example, the library modules described in later sections of this chapter provide
facilities for handling queues, sets, trees, tables, arrays and graphs. For such
high-level types, there is often no single representation which is obviously
the best.

Programs which use such a module not only call the functions provided,
but also store values of the given type. If programs process these values
directly rather than using the functions provided by the module, then the

programs are dependent on the particular representation chosen, and so the representation cannot be safely changed.

An **abstract type** (not to be confused with an algebraic type – see Section 2.3.3) is a type which is independent of any particular representation. The only way to process values of that type is to use the functions provided. The representation of an abstract type can be changed without any effect on programs which use it – the type is completely determined by the functions and their behaviour.

As an example, take the following implementation of two-dimensional vectors as pairs of numbers. The name *vector* is introduced as a synonym for pairs of numbers, and a small selection of functions is defined for creating vectors, finding their length, forming scalar multiples of them, adding them, and forming dot products:

```
vector   ==   (num, num)

vec a b  =   (a, b)
len (a,b)   =   sqrt (a^2 + b^2)
mul k (a,b)   =   (k*a,  k*b)
add (a,b) (c,d)   =   (a+c,  b+d)
dot (a,b) (c,d)   =   a*c + b*d
```

We want to make sure that a program which uses these functions cannot process them as pairs, e.g. by using pattern matching or the standard functions *fst* and *snd*. If we can accomplish this, then the representation can be changed at some future date. For example, we might want to enhance the package to handle three dimensions – two dimensional vectors might then be represented as triples with zero in the third component.

The feature which Miranda provides for accomplishing this is the **abstype** declaration which gives the name of the abstract type and lists the types of all those functions which are allowed to have access to the representation. To turn the above definitions into an abstract type, the following declaration can be added:

```
abstype   vector   with
    vec   ::   num->num->vector
    len   ::   vector->num
    mul   ::   num->vector->vector
    add   ::   vector->vector->vector
    dot   ::   vector->vector->num
```

This list of function types allows the compiler to tell which pairs of numbers in a program represent vectors, and which do not, so that *vector* and *(num, num)* can be treated as different types. The type system then prevents any functions other than the ones listed from accessing the representation of vectors.

The type definition *vector == (num, num)*, which was an inessential definition of a synonym before the addition of the **abstype** declaration, now becomes vital. It is needed by the abstract type mechanism to specify that the abstract type *vector* is being represented using pairs of numbers.

If one abstract type needs access to the representation of another, the types can be declared together – see Section 5.3.2 for an example. The **abstype** mechanism is independent of import and export – **abstype** declarations can occur anywhere in a script. However, it is often convenient to put an abstract type into its own module, with the **abstype** declaration near the beginning as part of the module interface, and with a %export declaration to avoid exporting the support functions from the module.

It is not meaningful to apply = or the other comparison operators to values of an abstract type. Depending on which implementation of Miranda you are using, this will either generate an error message, or it may produce an "unreliable" answer, depending on accidents of representation. Either way, you should not do it – if you want an equality test to be available on the abstract type, you should include an appropriately named function in its *abstype* declaration, and call it explicitly.

Also, applying the *show* function to a value of an abstract type will, by default, yield the string *""*. This behaviour can be modified, however, by including an appropriately named show function in the *abstype* declaration – see the Miranda manual for details.

## 4.2  Behaviour

We have already seen that if modules are to be developed independently, they must have simple, stable interfaces. The interface facilities in the previous section, as with any programming language, control the syntax of the interaction between modules. They control the names, the types and the visibility of the functions which are provided by one module for use in another. However, they do not specify the behaviour of the functions provided.

The behaviour of a module, as seen from the outside, also needs to be simple and stable. The behaviour needs to be simple so that the module can be easily understood and used correctly without having to worry about the internal details of its implementation. The behaviour needs to be stable, because any change in behaviour may involve investigating every call to the module made by every program which uses it to see if the module is still being used correctly. This is particularly important for a library module where the slightest change in behaviour may invalidate existing programs.

In this section, we briefly discuss three aspects of the behaviour of modules – how to specify what a module does, how to check that a module is sufficiently general, and how to measure or increase the efficiency of a module. There are few language features to support these activities, but they are just as important as the design of module interfaces.

## 4.2.1 Specification

One of the most important factors in module design is to provide, for users of a module, a simple and accurate description of what the module does. Such a description is called a **specification**. A specification may simply take the form of a comment at the beginning of a module, or it may include function definitions which provide a more precise description. The aim is to provide some accurate mental picture for the user, reinforced by consistent and evocative names for the functions provided.

One approach is to use analogies. For example, in the discussion of queues in Section 4.3 the analogy of human queues is used. In the set module in Section 4.4, there is a direct analogy with sets as used in mathematics.

A second approach which is somewhat more precise is to give properties of the functions in the module. For example, the action of a sorting function can be explained by saying that the result list contains the same members as the original list, i.e. is a permutation of it, and is ordered. It is possible to define these properties very precisely by providing definitions of functions which check them:

```
permutation xs ys  =  (xs--ys) = (ys--xs) = []

ordered []  =  True
ordered xs
=  and [x<=y | (x,y) <- zip2 xs (tl xs)]
```

Sometimes, a module may be open-ended, and the best you can do is to describe conventions which it adheres to. For example, consider a module which provides text handling facilities for use in processing portable text files – ones intended for transferring information between different application programs or different computers. You might define a type synonym:

```
line  ==  [char]
```

with the convention that a *line* contains no control characters or trailing spaces, and perhaps has a maximum length. It would not be appropriate to force these conventions on a programmer by declaring an abstract type, because a programmer would want to be able to use standard list processing functions on lines, and might want to break the conventions temporarily during processing. What is needed is a clear description of the conventions associated with use of the type synonym, perhaps supported by functions which convert lists of characters into lines or which check that the conventions hold.

Another possible approach to specification is to provide a **prototype** – a simple implementation which is written without regard for efficiency, but which conveys the ideas as clearly as possible. Such a prototype can kill two birds with one stone – it provides an initial implementation which can be used for demonstration and testing, and it acts as a specification for later implementations. As an example, a different way of specifying a sorting function is to give a simple prototype definition for it:

```
sort []  =  []
sort xs  =  min xs : sort (xs -- [min xs])
```

This says that the first member of the result is the smallest member of the original list, and the rest of the result is obtained by sorting the remainder of the original list. It is essentially the selection sort algorithm described in Section 4.2.3 below, but is unlikely to be efficient enough to be used as the final version of the *sort* function.

We will see in Chapter 5 that complete functional programs can themselves act as prototypes for large projects in which the final implementation is to be carried out in some other language.

## 4.2.2   Generality

Where the design of a library module is concerned, it is important to provide facilities which cover as wide a range of applications as possible. The distinguishing features of functional languages – polymorphism, laziness, and higher-order functions – make it relatively easy to do this. However, it is still important to check that functions cover all the cases that are likely to be required. We give here a few questions which you can ask about a function, and we illustrate by giving answers for the standard *sort* function.

Can a function be used on a sufficiently wide range of types? The type of *sort* is *[\*]->[\*]* which suggests that it can be used on lists of any type. However, *sort* relies on comparisons of members, so it does not work on lists of functions, and can only work on lists of infinite data values in special circumstances. This is as much as one can expect from a sorting function.

Can a function be used on streams or infinite lists? The *sort* function cannot, but then no sorting function could, because you have to scan the entire input list to find the minimum, i.e. the first member of the result.

Are there any variations or extensions which users might want? For *sort*, the most obvious extension is the ability to sort using something other than the standard comparison operators. There may be a case for a separate sorting module in which a comparison function is passed as an extra argument, or as a module parameter.

Can a function be adapted for a wide variety of uses? The standard sorting function is very flexible. For example, you might want to sort a list of people by age. If people are represented by *person* structures as in Section 2.3.3, then the standard *sort* function can be adapted for the purpose:

```
agesort ps
=  [p | (a,p) <- sort [(age p, p) | p<-ps]]
```

This attaches the age field separately to each person structure, sorts, and then removes the extra age field again. People with the same age are sorted by name.

### 4.2.3  Efficiency

Efficiency is perhaps the one aspect of the behaviour of a module which can be changed safely from one version of the module to another without affecting the correctness of programs which use the module.

Functional languages are important for investigating the effectiveness and correctness of algorithms, and for building prototypes. In such situations, efficiency is not usually the main issue. However, efficiency is an important factor in large application programs, or in the design of library modules – if a module is not efficient enough, nobody will want to use it.

The efficiency of a program involves both the time it takes and the space it uses. The space used is difficult to predict or measure, and we will only make a few comments about it, concentrating mostly on the time taken. When investigating the efficiency of a program, it is convenient to distinguish between two different issues – the complexity of the algorithm used and the speed of its implementation.

When operations are carried out on large data structures such as tables or trees, the most important issue is often the computational **complexity** of the algorithms used. This involves finding out how the time taken (or space used) by a function increases with problem size, ignoring constant factors. For example, functions on lists can be classified according to whether they take a constant amount of time like *hd* and *tl*, or an amount of time which rises linearly with the length of the input list like *map* or *filter*, or an amount of time which rises quadratically with the length of the list like *mkset* (which compares every member of a list to every other in order to remove duplicates) and so on.

The most effective way to make improvements in the efficiency of programs is often to replace algorithms or data structures by ones with better complexities. Re-engineering a program in this way is relatively easy if it has been properly divided into separate modules. The complexity of a function definition can be checked by timing the function when used on several different sizes of argument. However, the complexity of an algorithm can often be determined by an informal analysis, without implementing it in detail. As an example, we will analyse several different algorithms for sorting.

The recursive design principles described in Chapter 3 lead to four different sorting algorithms. Recursion on the input list leads to the insertion sort algorithm – sort the tail, then insert the head into the correct position. Recursion on the result list leads to the selection sort algorithm – find the minimum, then sort the remainder. Divide-and-conquer recursion on the input list leads to the merge sort algorithm – split the input list into two, sort the two parts separately, and merge the resulting ordered lists. Divide-and-conquer recursion on the result list leads to the quick sort algorithm – divide the input list into those members which are less than, and those which are greater than a certain "pivot" value, sort the two parts, and then concatenate the resulting lists. A suitable pivot value might be the middle member of the input list. See the definition of *sort* given in Appendix B, which uses the quick sort algorithm.

The selection sort algorithm is perhaps the easiest to analyse. One way to estimate the complexity of a recursive algorithm is to find out how long a call takes, excluding the time taken by any recursive calls, and then to find out how many recursive calls are made on a given problem. The time taken by a call to selection sort is essentially the time taken to find the minimum of the input list, which is proportional to its length. For a list of length $n$ there is one recursive call for a sublist of each length $n$, $n\text{-}1$, $n\text{-}2$, ... making *n* calls with an average length of *n/2*. The total time is thus proportional to *n^2*, i.e. quadratic in *n*.

The insertion sort algorithm is similar, except that the time taken to insert the head into the sorted tail may take less than linear time, depending on how far into the tail it has to be inserted. For random lists, the head is inserted half way along the tail on average, so insertion takes linear time, and the algorithm as a whole is quadratic. However, if the input list is already nearly ordered, so that each member is no more than some fixed distance away from its correct position, then in each recursive call, the head is inserted a maximum of the same fixed distance into the tail. Insertion thus takes a constant amount of time, and the algorithm as a whole is linear in this case.

The merge sort algorithm can be analysed as follows. The time taken by a call, excluding recursive calls, is linear – it is the time taken to merge two half-length ordered sublists. The recursive calls made on a list of length *n* are as follows. First there is a call on the whole list taking, say, *n* steps. Then there are two calls on lists of length *n/2* taking *n/2* steps each, making a total of *n* steps. Then there are *4* calls on lists of length *n/4*, again taking a total of *n* steps. Thus the calls for any particular length of sublist take a total of *n* steps, and the lengths are *n*, *n/2*, *n/4*, etc. The number of different lengths is the number of times *n* can be divided by *2*, which is the logarithm of *n* to the base *2*. Where complexity is concerned, the base of logarithms is unimportant, so we can just say that the number of different lengths is proportional to *log n*. Thus the total time taken by the merge sort algorithm is proportional to *n \* log n*, making it superior to any quadratic algorithm on long lists, since *log n* grows slowly with *n*.

The quick sort algorithm can be analysed in a similar way to merge sort. The only difference is that when the input list is divided into two parts using a pivot value, the two parts are not necessarily the same length. Nevertheless, quick sort works well on random lists, and choosing the middle member as a pivot means that it works well on lists which are nearly ordered already. In fact, quick sort takes a time proportional to *n \* log n* in all but the most pathological of cases.

Now let us turn to the question of the **speed** of the implementation of an algorithm. The speed is taken to be the constant factor ignored when discussing complexity. For example, a better implementation may double the efficiency of a function, without changing the complexity. This is most important when a function is used frequently on small arguments.

Unfortunately, the speed of implementation depends critically on the computer and compiler being used, and is mostly a matter of skill and experiment. Some hints are: simple definitions are usually better than complicated ones, and definitions using standard tools with built-in optimised implementations are often better than direct recursive definitions. However, predicting the speed of an implementation is difficult, and measurement is often the only practical approach.

The Miranda system provides some simple tools for measuring the time or space which a program uses. The main tool is the command `/count` which switches on measurement of the number of steps taken and memory cells allocated during the running of programs. However, the results obtained have to be interpreted with care.

You must bear in mind that a lot of time and space is often taken up in formatting and printing results. If you arrange for the result not to be printed, e.g. by asking for the length of a list rather than the list itself, then the laziness of the language makes it difficult to be sure that the relevant values have actually been evaluated at all. There are standard functions `seq` and `force` which can be used to help overcome this problem by changing evaluation order. For example, to check on the resources used in evaluating a value `result`, you can evaluate the expression:

    ?  seq (force result) "Done"

This evaluates `result` without printing its value, and then prints *Done*. The `seq` function ensures that evaluation of its first argument begins before evaluation of its second argument, and returns its second argument. The `force` function ensures that its argument is fully evaluated before returning it. The use of these functions is rather subtle, so they should be used sparingly. One other use for them is in interactive programs (see Chapter 5) to ensure that operating system operations occur in the right order.

Another problem is the fact that functional languages use a heap and a garbage collector (see Chapter 7) for data storage. This means that the total number of memory cells allocated is not as important as the maximum number of cells which are active at any time – a figure which is difficult to determine. One trick which can be used is to reduce the total amount of heap space available and compare programs to see which of them run out of space altogether.

The issues of complexity and speed often conflict, and compromise algorithms are needed to give the best all round performance. For example, for sorting long lists, merge sort and quick sort have better complexities than the others. On the other hand, insertion sort, because of its simplicity, can often be implemented so as to work faster on short lists – and it has better complexity on nearly ordered lists. A compromise algorithm which combines quick sort and insertion sort can be designed as follows. Use quick sort first, but stop when the sublists are less than some fixed size. The result of this is a nearly ordered list – the correct position of each member is somewhere in its own sublist. Use insertion sort on this nearly ordered list to finish the job.

## 4.3 Queues

Human queues are very familiar. You join the back of a queue, wait until you get to the front, and then you are dealt with and leave. This analogy provides a valuable picture of the behaviour of queues in computing – they are used to store a collection of values waiting to be processed when the order of processing must be "first come first served". An interface for a queue module can be defined by:

```
%export queue emptyqueue join front leave

abstype   queue  *   with
    emptyqueue   ::   queue  *
    join         ::   queue  * -> * -> queue  *
    front        ::   queue  * -> *
    leave        ::   queue  * -> queue  *
```

The %export declaration exports the name of the abstract type and all the operations on it.

The easiest way to specify the exact behaviour of queues is to give a prototype implementation in which queues are represented as lists with the beginning of the list acting as the front of the queue and the end of the list acting as the back of the queue:

```
queue  *   ==   [*]

emptyqueue  =  []
join q x  =   q ++ [x]
front q  =   hd q
leave q  =   tl q
```

The item at the beginning of the list can be examined with *front*, and then removed with *leave*. It would also be possible to have a single function returning both the front item and the adjusted queue, but we have chosen to have two separate functions.

This implementation is fine for many purposes, but there is an efficiency problem for long queues. The *join* function takes an amount of time proportional to the length of the queue, because the queue has to be scanned and copied before attaching the new item to the end. We would like an alternative implementation, with exactly the same behaviour, in which each of the queue operations takes a constant amount of time.

There is a clever implementation of queues as pairs of lists in which each queue operation takes constant time on average. It is somewhat similar to the "circular array" technique in procedural languages (Sedgewick [13]), or the "difference list" technique in logic languages (Sterling & Shapiro [15]).

The trick is to represent a queue as a pair of lists *(xs,ys)*, say, in which *xs* represents the items at the front of the queue, and *ys* represents the items at the back:

$$queue \; * \;\; == \;\; ([*],[*])$$

The list *ys* is held in reverse order so that *join* can be implemented efficiently. Thus the queue <1,2,3,4,5,6,7> might be represented as the pair *([1,2,3],[7,6,5,4])*. The representation is not unique – it depends on the history of accesses.

The empty queue is just a pair of empty lists. To make sure that the *front* function always takes a constant time, we keep to the convention that every non-empty queue must have a non-empty front list. For example, the representation *([], [7,6,5,4,3,2,1])* for the queue above is ruled out. Then the *front* function can just return the first member of the first list:

$$emptyqueue \;\; = \;\; ([],[])$$
$$front \; (x:rxs,ys) \;\; = \;\; x$$

The *join* function adds an item to a non-empty queue by putting it at the back, i.e. at the beginning of the second list. For an empty queue, the item must be put in the first list, because of the above convention. In any case, *join* clearly takes constant time:

$$join \; ([],[]) \; z \;\; = \;\; ([z],[])$$
$$join \; (xs,ys) \; z \;\; = \;\; (xs,z:ys)$$

Finally, the *leave* function removes the first member of the first list. However, if that makes the first list empty, the second list must be reversed and used to replace the first one:

```
leave (x:rxs,ys)
=   (rxs,ys),              if rxs ~= []
=   (reverse ys, []),   if rxs = []
```

The *leave* function takes more than constant time when *rxs* is empty, because the time taken by the call to the standard *reverse* function is proportional to the length of the list *ys*. However, we can show that *leave* takes a constant time on average. Suppose *leave* moves *100* items from *ys* to *xs* taking, say, one step per item. Then the next *100* calls to *leave* will remove those *100* items at only one step per call. Thus in the sequence of calls as a whole, each call takes an average of about two steps.

Looking at it another way, any particular item will typically be moved from *ys* to *xs* once, contributing one step to a call of *leave*, and will be removed from *xs* once, contributing one step to a second call of *leave*. Thus in passing *n* items through the queue, *leave* will be called *n* times, taking a total of *2*n* steps, giving an average of *2* steps per call, as before.

## 4.4   Sets

A **set** is a collection of values in which order is unimportant and which contains no duplicates. Sets should be familiar from mathematics, but the set module presented here only supports finite sets. The elements of a set can be finite values of any data type – this relies on the fact that any such values can be compared using the standard comparison operators =, < etc. We can provide an interface for the set module as follows:

```
%export set setof list in emptyset insert
         union intersect difference disjoint

abstype  set *  with
    setof         ::  [*] -> set *
    list          ::  set * -> [*]
    in            ::  set * -> * -> bool
    emptyset      ::  set *
    insert        ::  set * -> * -> set *
    union         ::  set * -> set * -> set *
    intersect     ::  set * -> set * -> set *
    difference    ::  set * -> set * -> set *
    disjoint      ::  set * -> set * -> bool
```

As a prototype implementation, sets can be represented as ordered lists containing no duplicates:

```
set *  ==  [*]


setof xs  =  unique (sort xs)
list xs  =  xs
in xs x  =  member xs x
emptyset  =  setof []
insert xs x  =  union xs [x]
union xs ys  =  unique (merge xs ys)
intersect xs ys  =  [x | x<-xs; in ys x]
difference xs ys  =  xs -- ys
disjoint xs ys  =  intersect xs ys = emptyset


unique []  =  []
unique [x]  =  [x]
unique (x0:x1:rxs)
=  unique (x1:rxs),       if x0=x1
=  x0 : unique (x1:rxs),  otherwise
```

The *setof* function converts a list into a set, *list* converts a set into a list – an ordered one with no duplicates, *in* tests whether a value is an element of a set, and *emptyset* is the set with no elements. The *insert* function adds a new element to a set. The *union* function forms the union of two sets using the standard *merge* function and the support function *unique*. Both *merge* and *unique* take linear time, and so *union* is linear too – it takes an amount of time proportional to the total length of its arguments.

The *intersect* and *difference* functions are given simple definitions which take quadratic time – they can be improved to take linear time (see the exercises).

The *unique* function is a support function which removes duplicates from an ordered list by comparing adjacent members. It does not appear in the %export declaration at the beginning of the module, so programs which include the set module cannot use it.

There is no single best way to implement sets, and so an efficient implementation is usually chosen depending on the way in which sets are to be used. The implementation above is useful when a wide range of set operations is needed, or when set operations are infrequent, or when efficiency is not essential. If all the sets handled in a program are subsets of some fixed, finite set, then they might be represented as arrays of booleans. If *insert* and *in* are the most frequent operations, then a table implementation might be appropriate. If disjoint unions are frequent, then a representation using trees might be the most efficient. If infinite sets need to be implemented, they can be represented as boolean functions (see the exercises), though only some of the set operations described above can be supported.

## 4.5 Trees

Trees are very common in computer science for representing hierarchically structured data. One important application is in representing syntactic structures, as we shall see in Chapter 6. For example, the structure of a Miranda equation such as *f x y = (x, y)* can be captured very clearly in a tree diagram in which the symbols =, @ and p are used to mark equations, function applications, and pairs respectively. Trees are usually drawn upside down in computer science, as with family trees:

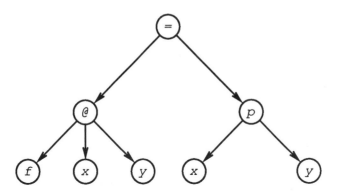

The terminology used for trees comes from a variety of sources. Like more general graphs (see Section 4.8), a **tree** is a collection of **nodes**, each having a **label** and a number of **edges** pointing to other nodes. Like a family tree, a node is called the **parent** of its **children**, which are **siblings** of each other. Like a natural tree, a tree structure consists of a **root** node with **branches** leading to its subtrees, and a node with no subtrees is called a **leaf** node.

A new type can be introduced to represent a tree as a structure built with a new constructor *Tree*, say. The structure contains two fields, one for the root label and one for the list of subtrees. Trees are polymorphic, since the labels can be of any type:

```
tree *   ::=   Tree * [tree *]
```

With this representation, the syntax tree shown above can be represented as a tree with strings stored in the labels:

```
Tree "=" [
  Tree "@" [Tree "f" [], Tree "x" [], Tree "y" []],
  Tree "p" [Tree "x" [], Tree "y" []]
]
```

The operations defined on tree structures depend rather radically on the application, and so it is usual not to define a general abstract type for trees, but rather to define tree types of various kinds as needed. We will just describe a few simple functions on trees which illustrate some of the ideas used in implementing tree operations.

The *size* function is one of the simplest examples of operations which involve scanning a tree. It counts the number of nodes in a tree by adding one (for the root node) to the sum of the sizes of the subtrees:

```
size (Tree lb sts)  =  1 + sum [size t | t<-sts]
```

This function takes linear time, i.e. a time proportional to the number of nodes in the tree. There is one call per node. The amount of time taken by the call, excluding the time for recursive calls, is proportional to the number of subnodes of that node. Thus the total time taken by *size* is proportional to the total number of subnodes in the tree. Since each node is a subnode of only one other node (except for the root), this is also the total number of nodes in the tree.

In more complicated tree operations, it is often necessary to define a support function which operates on a list of subtrees. For example, consider the problem of attaching a unique number to each node of a tree, by replacing each label *lb* with a pair *(n, lb)*. A function *attach* can be defined which takes a number *n* and a tree, and returns the new tree with consecutive numbers from *n* upwards attached to the nodes. A support function *attachs* is used to attach numbers to a list of subtrees:

```
attach n (Tree lb sts)
=  Tree (n,lb) (attachs (n+1) sts)

attachs n []  =  []
attachs n (t:rts)
=  attach n t : attachs (n + size t) rts
```

The function *attach* takes a time which is greater than linear, because it calls the *size* function once for every subtree. Each node takes part in a call to *size* for each subtree in which it appears, i.e. once for each node above it in the path up the tree to the root. Thus the time taken per node is proportional to its distance from the root. The average distance from the root in a tree with *n* nodes is *log n* for all but the most pathological of trees, since trees generally branch out exponentially. Thus the total time taken for *attach* is proportional to *n * log n* rather than being linear as we would hope. However, since *log n* grows very slowly with *n*, this is not much worse than linear.

It is possible to define a version of *attach* which takes linear time by returning a pair containing the size of the subtree as well as the processed tree (and similarly for *attachs*), thus effectively combining the size and attachment computations in a single pass over the tree. However, with the extra complication involved, the new version is likely to be less efficient on small trees, and only significantly more efficient on very large trees.

Perhaps the simplest operation which converts a tree into a linear form is the *flatten* function which extracts the list of all the labels in a tree. It returns the root label, followed by the concatenation of the lists of labels in the subtrees:

```
flatten (Tree lb sts)
=   lb : concat [flatten t | t<-sts]
```

As with *attach*, this definition takes a time proportional to *n * log n* on a tree with *n* nodes, since each node is involved in several calls of *concat*.

In cases like this it is possible to define a linear version of the function by adding an extra argument called a **continuation** used to determine where to continue the traversal of the tree after the processing of the current subtree has been completed. In the case of *flatten*, a new version *flatten'* can be defined which takes an extra continuation argument *cn* representing a list of labels to be produced after the ones in the current tree. In other words, *flatten' t cn* is equivalent to *(flatten t) ++ cn*. The definition of *flatten'* uses a support function *flats*, with a similar continuation argument, to take the place of the use of *concat*.

```
flatten' (Tree lb sts) cn  =   lb : flats sts cn

flats [] cn  =  cn
flats (t:rts) cn  =  flatten' t (flats rts cn)
```

The function *flats* calls *flatten'* on the first subtree, passing it a continuation indicating that after the first subtree has been flattened, processing should continue by calling *flats* on the remaining subtrees. When *flats* finishes, it passes control to its own continuation. As before, this new version of *flatten* may only be an improvement on large trees.

When experimenting with trees, it is useful to have a show function which can be used to print them out in a textual form which reveals their structure. One way of doing this is to print a tree on several lines, with a label on each line and with indenting to indicate the levels of the tree. For example, if a tree represents the hierarchical relationships of the parts of a book, then printing the tree out in this way corresponds roughly to a table of contents:

```
book
    chapter1
        section1.1
        section1.2
            subsection1.2.1
        section1.3
    chapter2
        section2.1
    ...
```

We can define a function *showtree* which takes as its first argument a function for showing labels, and as its second the tree to be shown. It is defined in terms of a function *indent* which converts a tree into a list of indented lines. The *indent* function converts each subtree into a list of lines, and then concatenates these lists, adding an extra level of indenting to every line:

```
showtree f t  =  lay (indent f t)

indent f (Tree lb sts)
= f lb : ["   " ++ cs | t<-sts; cs <- indent f t]
```

The *indent* function is rather like *flatten*, except that we have chosen to use a list comprehension with two generators instead of *concat*. It takes a time proportional to $n * log\ n$ on a tree with $n$ nodes and, as with *flatten*, it can be made linear by adding an extra continuation argument.

## 4.6 Tables

A **table** is a collection of entries in which a key is used to find some associated value. For example, in a telephone directory, a person's name is used as a key to find their telephone number. The entries can be represented by pairs such as:

```
("Chris", "123")
("Pat", "456")
("Bill", "999")
```

The main operations required on tables are to look up an entry and to update a table by adding or changing an entry. It is also convenient to include operations to load up a table from a given list of pairs and to extract the contents of a table as a list of pairs. Thus, an interface for a table module, treating tables as an abstract type, might be:

```
%export table lookup update tableof entries

abstype table * **  with
    lookup  ::  table * ** -> * -> ** -> **
    update  ::  table * ** -> * -> ** -> table * **
    tableof ::  [(*,**)] -> table * **
    entries ::  table * ** -> [(*,**)]
```

A natural efficient implementation in a procedural language would be to use a structure such as an array or hash table which supports update in place, which would make lookup a constant time operation. As mentioned in Section 2.6, current pure functional languages often do not support data structures which can be updated in place, so we have to look for other implementation methods.

As a prototype implementation, we can represent a table as a list of pairs, with the most recent entries at the front. Such lists are often called **association lists**:

```
table * **  ==  [(*,**)]

lookup t x d  =  hd ([v | (k,v)<-t; k=x] ++ [d])
update t x y  =  (x,y) : [(k,v) | (k,v)<-t; k~=x]
tableof es  =  es
entries t  =  sort t
```

The *update* function adds an entry to the beginning of the list, and removes
any old entries with the same key. The *lookup* function finds the pair with
a given key and returns the associated value. It returns a given default value
*d* if there is no entry with the given key. The *tableof* function creates a
new table from a list, assuming that the keys are unique, i.e. no two pairs
have the same key. The *entries* function returns the pairs in the list. For
tables to form a true abstract type, we have to ensure that *entries* returns
the pairs in a fixed order, regardless of the representation chosen for tables.
The definition above uses the standard *sort* function to ensure that they
are ordered by key.

With this implementation, *update* and *lookup* are linear time operations. The *update* function can be made to take constant time by attaching
the new pair to the beginning of the list without removing any old entries
with the given key. This does not affect *lookup* because it uses the first pair
it finds – the old ones simply become inaccessible. However, the *entries*
function would then have to remove all such out-of-date pairs.

To make the implementation of *lookup* more efficient in the absence of
data structures which can be updated in place, we can use binary trees. A
**binary tree** (see Sedgewick [13]) is a tree in which there can be at most two
branches coming out of a node, called the left and right branches. Binary
trees are not just a special case of general trees, because if there is only one
branch, it can either be a lone left branch or a lone right branch – these two
cases cannot be distinguished in general trees. Binary trees use an explicit
empty subtree marker to represent this extra information:

$$bin \ * \quad ::= \quad Empty \ | \ Fork \ (bin \ *) \ * \ (bin \ *)$$

A binary tree is either *Empty*, or is a structure built with the *Fork* constructor and having three fields: a left subtree, a label, and a right subtree.
Either subtree of a node may be *Empty*.

When binary trees are used to implement tables, each label is a table
entry and the entries are kept in order by key. The left subtree at a node
contains only entries with smaller keys than the entry in the node, and the
right subtree contains only entries with larger keys. Binary trees used in
this way are called **binary search trees**. When searching for an entry, a
key comparison at each node determines which subtree to search in.

The shape of the tree is unimportant – it is determined by the history of
accesses. For example, one of the possible ways in which the letters *dgmnopr*
might be stored in a binary search tree is:

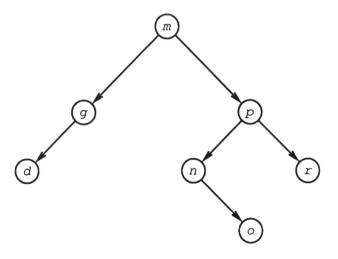

The *lookup* and *update* operations can be defined using binary search trees by:

```
table * **   ==  bin (*,**)

lookup Empty k d  =  d
lookup (Fork left e right) k d
=   lookup left k d,    if k < fst e
=   snd e,              if k = fst e
=   lookup right k d,   if k > fst e

update Empty k v  =  Fork Empty (k,v) Empty
update (Fork left e right) k v
=   Fork (update left k v) e right,   if k < fst e
=   Fork left (k,v) right,            if k = fst e
=   Fork left e (update right k v),   if k > fst e
```

These *lookup* and *update* operations both take an amount of time proportional to *log n* for a tree with *n* entries, provided that the tree is well-balanced, i.e. has a depth which is proportional to *log n*. If items are entered into a binary tree in a random order, then the tree is balanced. Unfortunately, the order of entry is often far from random, in which case the binary tree implementation is rather poor. There are various schemes which can be used to keep a binary tree balanced (see Sedgewick [13]), but these complicate the implementation somewhat.

Instead, the problem of poorly balanced trees can be counteracted by defining the *tableof* function so that it produces a perfectly balanced tree

from a given list of entries. It can be used to create or initialise a table or,
in conjunction with *entries*, to re-balance a table when it is found to have
become unbalanced:

```
tableof es
=  build (sort es)  where
   build es
   =  Empty,                   if es=[]
   =  Fork left (es!m) right,  otherwise
      where
      left  =  build (take m es)
      right =  build (drop (m+1) es)
      m  =  #es div 2
```

It is worth providing a second version *lazy_tableof* of the *tableof*
function. Of course, the module interface needs to be adapted to accommo-
date it. This second version can be used when a table needs to be lazy, e.g.
if it is created from a stream of information supplied interactively by the
user. The following definition ensures that if a key is looked up in the table,
the argument list *es* is only evaluated as far as the relevant entry:

```
lazy_tableof []    =  Empty
lazy_tableof (e:res)
=  Fork left e right
   where
   left  =  lazy_tableof (filter (<e) res)
   right =  lazy_tableof (filter (>e) res)
```

Finally, the *entries* function returns the entries in order by key. At
each node, it returns the entries in the left subtree, followed by the entry in
the node, followed by the entries in the right subtree:

```
entries Empty  =  []
entries (Fork left e right)
=  entries left ++ [e] ++ entries right
```

This implementation of tables is sufficiently general to be used in a wide
variety of situations. For example, suppose that several values can be associated with the same key, e.g. several phone numbers associated with the
same name. The implementation above appears to allow only one entry with
a given key. However, we can create a table in which each name is paired
with a list of numbers, e.g. *("Sam", [246,357])*.

Another variation is when we want entries other than pairs. For example, we might want to store a collection of structures of type *person*, as introduced in Section 2.3.3, with a person's name being used as the key. In this case, a table can be defined in which a copy of the name field is paired with each structure, e.g. *("Chris", Person "Chris" 18 Female)*. Alternatively, the implementation can easily be adapted so that the entries are the structures themselves by replacing the uses of the standard functions *fst* and *snd* in the definitions of *update* and *lookup*.

## 4.7 Arrays

Arrays are often not directly supported in current pure functional languages, because of the problems of updating in place, and in particular they are not supported in the version of Miranda on which this book is based. In this section, we describe methods for implementing a module in Miranda which provides the same facilities as arrays, although not with the same efficiency.

Arrays are often used in procedural programs only because other data structures are less convenient – most of the applications of arrays can be handled in a much cleaner way in functional languages using lists or other data types. Nevertheless, there are occasional situations in which it is natural to think in terms of arrays, or in which the efficiency which arrays can provide is important, and so it is convenient to provide a prototype module which supports array operations, though not constant time ones.

One approach is to treat an array as a table in which the keys form a fixed sequence of numbers, say *[0..n]*, and indeed the implementation of tables as binary trees described in the previous section can be used. Since the collection of indexes is fixed, the shape of the tree does not change once it has been initialised, and initialising the array with *tableof* will ensure that the tree is well-balanced. The operations thus take a time proportional to *log n* for arrays of length *n*, regardless of the sequence of accesses.

It is not possible to find an implementation with a better complexity than this without help from some built-in language feature supporting update in place, but it may be possible to improve the speed of the implementation a little. One simple way to implement array operations is to represent an array as a list *xs*, index into the list using the standard *!* operator, and update it using the standard functions *take* and *drop*. The lookup and update operations would then take linear time, but they are likely be more efficient than binary tree operations for short arrays, particularly if the compiler optimises the use of the *!* operator.

A compromise between the tree and list implementations is also possible, by storing the array items in short lists in the leaf nodes of a variation on a binary tree – see the exercises. This compromise is similar to **B-trees** (see Sedgewick [13]) which are used in databases.

The implementation of tables and arrays is one of the few areas where operations cannot be defined in functional languages with the same complexity as in procedural languages without updating in place. The introduction of such update facilities into functional languages allows constant time table and array operations to be defined. Optimisation techniques which allow update in place to be implemented efficiently in pure functional languages are discussed in Section 6.5.3.

## 4.8   Graphs

When structures with cross-references are required in a procedural language, they are usually implemented using pointers. However, pointers are to data what jumps are to code – their indiscriminate use can lead to "spaghetti" programs whose logic is impossible to follow. Moreover, pointers change dynamically, and it can take considerable self-discipline when programming to ensure that they remain consistent.

In pure functional languages, pointers are not directly accessible to programmers – pointers are used in the implementation as abbreviations for the values they point to. This clean approach means that data structures must be tree-like, and cannot contain direct cross-references. For example, if you define what looks like a cyclic data structure, you find that it is indistinguishable from an infinite tree (see the exercises).

Graphs are structures which are used to record relationships between values in a setting where arbitrary cross-references are allowed, just as trees record relationships between values in a hierarchical setting. A **graph** is a collection of labelled nodes, together with a collection of edges, each edge representing a reference from one node to another. Such graphs are sometimes called **directed** graphs or **networks**. An example of a graph is:

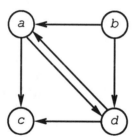

As a simple prototype implementation, a graph can be represented as a pair consisting of a list of nodes and a list of edges. Each edge is a pair of nodes. Strictly speaking, a graph should consist of a set of nodes and a set of edges, but it is often convenient to use the extra ordering information implicit in the lists. The representation of the above graph might be:

$$([a,b,c,d], \quad [(a,c),(a,d),(b,a),(b,d),(d,a),(d,c)])$$

This representation assumes that the node labels are all distinct, so that they can be used as names for the nodes. For example, the above representation could be completed by adding definitions such as $a = "a"$ which provide strings as node names. Thus an edge contains the name of a node, rather than pointing directly to it, which effectively inserts an extra level of indirection compared to a pointer implementation. This allows for arbitrary cross-referencing including **cycles**, i.e. circular sequences of cross-references as formed by $a$ and $d$ in the above example.

The most important operation which a graph module must provide is a function $out$, say, which produces a list of the nodes to which a given node points – its **neighbours**. It may also be convenient to have a function $invert$ which allows the edges to be followed in the reverse direction – it produces a new graph in which all the edges are reversed:

```
graph *    ==   ([*],[(*,*)])

nodes (ns,es)  =   ns
edges (ns,es)  =   es
out (ns,es) n  =   [n2 | (n1,n2)<-es; n1=n]
invert (ns,es) =   (ns, [(n2,n1) | (n1,n2)<-es])
```

The $out$ and $invert$ functions take linear time. In a language allowing tables with constant time lookup, a more efficient representation would involve a table with an entry for each node giving the list of neighbours of that node. The $out$ function would then take constant time, while $invert$ could still be defined as a linear operation.

Basic functions such as these can be collected into a module and protected by an **abstype** declaration, and then the module can be used to implement graph algorithms. As an example, we will present one common graph algorithm, namely depth first search. This algorithm can be used in a variety of applications, including dependency analysis which is discussed in Chapter 6.

A **depth first search** of a graph finds all the nodes which can be reached from a given starting node. The algorithm finds everything reachable from the first edge out of any node before moving on to the second, and so searches as deeply as possible into the graph before backtracking. By ignoring edges which go to nodes which have already been visited, the search determines a tree within the graph which joins up all the reachable nodes.

We generalise this slightly by defining a function *search* which takes a graph and a list of nodes and, for each node, finds the new nodes reachable from it, if any. It returns a list of trees. It works by scanning the given list of nodes with *foldl*, accumulating a pair of values consisting of the set of nodes visited so far, together with the list of trees constructed so far. The support function *searchnode* finds the new nodes reachable from a given node, if any, updating the set of visited nodes and the list of trees. It works by scanning the list of neighbours of the given node:

```
search g ns
=  snd (foldl searchnode (emptyset,[]) ns)   where

   searchnode (vs,ts) n
   =   (vs,ts),                    if in vs n
   =   (vs',(Tree n ts'):ts),     otherwise
       where
       (vs',ts')
       =  foldl searchnode (insert vs n, []) (out g n)
```

This algorithm, which is quite subtle, uses the *out* function from the graph module, *emptyset*, *insert* and *in* from the set module and the *Tree* constructor from the tree module. The algorithm is designed so that if update in place can be used to implement *insert* and *in* as constant time operations, then the time taken by *search* is linear in the number of edges.

The nodes in the resulting list of trees are in the reverse of the order in which the calls to *searchnode* are completed. Many depth first search algorithms use this ordering of the nodes. For example, in a simple job scheduling application, each node represents a job, and each edge *(a,b)* represents the fact that job *a* must be done before job *b*. The graph contains no cycles, and a suitable order in which to do the jobs can be found by:

```
schedule g
=   concat [flatten t | t <- search g (nodes g)]
```

If *search* is linear, and *flatten* is linear as discussed in Section 4.5, then *schedule* is also linear.

## 4.9 Exercises

1. Design a module for complex numbers represented as pairs of the type *(num, num)*. Use an **abstype** declaration to hide the representation.

2. Instead of defining queues as an abstract type, suppose they are defined as an algebraic type *queue \* ::= Q ([\*], [\*])* using a constructor *Q* to ensure that that the *queue* type is different from its representation type. To what extent does this prevent programs from accessing the representation of queues?

3. Define linear time versions of the *intersect* and *difference* functions on sets.

4. Design a module to handle infinite sets in which a set is represented as a boolean function which returns *True* when applied to one its elements, and *False* otherwise. For example, the set of even integers might be represented by the function:

   *even n* = *n* **mod** 2 = 0

   Implement versions of the functions *in*, *union*, *intersect* and *difference* which accept such functions as arguments representing infinite sets.

   Implement an operation which converts an ordered infinite list into an infinite set. Why is it not possible, in general, to convert an unordered infinite list into an infinite set, or an infinite set into a list?

5. Define a function *maptree* which takes a function *f* and a tree *t* and creates a new tree with the same structure as *t* by applying the function *f* to every label. Define a function *mirror* which forms the mirror image of a tree.

6. Define a function *leftmost* which takes a binary search tree and returns a pair consisting of the leftmost entry in the tree, and a new version of the tree with this leftmost entry removed. Use *leftmost* to define a function *graft* which takes two search trees *l* and *r* for which all the entries in *l* have smaller keys than any of the entries in *r*, and which joins these two trees into a single tree with the leftmost entry of *r* in its root. Finally, use *graft* to design a function *remove* which takes a tree and a key, and removes the entry with that key, if any, from the tree.

7. Design a prototype assembler which takes a stream of instructions interspersed with label definitions and returns a similar stream with all references to labels converted into memory locations. Use the function *lazy_tableof* to create a table containing the locations of all the labels. By applying the assembler to an instruction stream typed in interactively, show that the assembler is a stream function, i.e. that it does not read in any more of the input stream than is needed in order to deal with forward references.

8. Define array operations, similar to the operations on tables, using binary trees in which items are stored only in lists in the leaf nodes, using the algebraic type:

$$bin * ::= List [*] | Fork (bin *) num (bin *)$$

Each internal node contains a number against which the array index can be compared. If the index is less than this number, the left branch is taken. If the index is greater than or equal to the number, then the number is subtracted from the index and the right branch is taken. When a leaf node is reached, list operations are used as described in Section 4.7. Determine the length of list for which this compromise implementation works best on your computer.

9. In an attempt to produce an implementation closer to procedural pointer implementations of graphs, suppose a graph is represented as a list of nodes, and a node as a pair consisting of a label and a list of neighbour nodes. An example graph in this representation is:

```
triangle
=   [a,b,c]  where
     a  =   ("a",[b])
     b  =   ("b",[c])
     c  =   ("c",[a])
```

Does *triangle* represent a finite value or an infinite one? With this representation, is it possible to write a function *rename* which takes a graph and two node labels *n1* and *n2*, finds the node with label *n1* and changes its label to *n2* in such a way that all references to the node "see" the change?

# Chapter 5

# The Design of Programs

Writing a program involves designing a solution to the overall problem, working out how the solution can be split cleanly into a number of modules, and using the techniques of the previous chapter to develop the modules. This chapter describes the extra language features and programming techniques needed in the design of large programs, and provides three example programs.

The first section deals with the operating system interface, giving more details of input and output facilities than have been described up to now. The second section covers interactive programs, including line interaction, character interaction, and the handling of global data.

The remaining three sections provide examples of complete programs which use the techniques described in the earlier sections and which illustrate the process of program design. The first is a personal notebook program which demonstrates how permanent information can be stored in files from one program run to the next. The second is a simulation of a telephone exchange which illustrates how a functional program can act both as a specification and prototype for a large project. The final program is a simple expert system which involves algorithms usually associated with logic programming, and which shows how less conventional problems can be solved.

## 5.1 The Operating System Interface

A complete program must communicate with the computer's operating system in order to do input and output, interact with the user, or make use of external software or hardware facilities.

Unfortunately, almost all operating systems currently in existence are inherently procedural and are designed to support procedural programs. Such programs usually communicate with the operating system through procedure calls. Functional programs cannot usually be linked with procedure libraries, at least not without compromising the purity of the language, and in any case the procedure libraries provided differ from one operating system to another.

To counteract these problems, Miranda provides a number of facilities for interfacing to the host operating system in different ways, and the reader is referred to the Miranda system manual for details. In this section we introduce some standard input and output facilities which are used in the rest of the chapter.

### 5.1.1  Input

As mentioned briefly in Section 2.6.2, there is a function *read* for reading from files. A call such as *read "data"* returns the contents of a file called *data* as a stream of characters. For example, a program might contain the definition:

```
    input  =  lines (read "data")
```

The symbol *$-* can be regarded as a special case of this – it returns the standard input. This is usually the stream of characters typed at the keyboard during a program run, but the operating system may provide a means of taking the standard input from some other source. The stream can usually be terminated by some end-of-input convention provided by the operating system for terminating keyboard input (often CONTROL-D or CONTROL-Z).

There is also a special symbol *$+* which is like *$-*, except that it reads in a stream of values of any type instead of a stream of characters, with the values being typed in one per line. For details of these and other input facilities, see the Miranda system manual.

### 5.1.2  Output

With simple programs, output is carried out by evaluating an expression, the value of which is sent to the standard output, i.e. to the screen. To cope with more complicated output requirements, Miranda allows system messages to be sent to the operating system. A standard type *sys_message* is provided for storing system messages. The type is an algebraic one, as if given by a definition of the form:

```
sys_message
::=  Stdout [char] | Tofile [char] [char] | ...
```

The most important system messages are *Stdout cs* which sends the stream of characters *cs* to the standard output, which is usually the screen, and *Tofile filename cs*, which sends *cs* to the given file. For details of kinds of system messages other than the two described here, see the Miranda system manual.

A value of type *sys_message* is an ordinary structure which can be processed in any of the usual ways. The only time when structures of this type are treated specially is when a list of them is evaluated. Then, instead of being printed on the screen, they are sent to the operating system to be processed. For example, the evaluation:

```
?  [Tofile "data" "line 1\nline 2\n", Stdout "Done"]
```

first creates a two-line file called *data* and then prints *Done* on the screen.

The usual conventions for printing the results of an evaluation can be regarded as abbreviations. A result expression *cs*, say, of type *[char]* is sent directly to the standard output unchanged, so the evaluation:

```
?  cs
```

can be regarded as an abbreviation for the evaluation:

```
?  [Stdout cs]
```

A result expression *x*, say, of any type other than the two types *[char]* or *[sys_message]* is converted into a list of characters with the standard *show* function and then sent to the standard output, so the evaluation:

```
?  x
```

can be regarded as an abbreviation for:

```
?  [Stdout (show x)]
```

For most programs, it is sufficient to output a complete file with a single *Tofile* message by putting the entire contents into its second field. However, for more complicated applications, it may be necessary to interleave output to the file with other output operations. To accomplish this, you are allowed to have many *Tofile* messages for the same file in the *sys_message* list. The first *Tofile* message creates (or over-writes) the output file and leaves it open for writing. Subsequent *Tofile* messages than add to what is in the file, and the file is closed when the program terminates. Similarly, there can be many *Stdout* messages in the list, so that output to the screen can be interleaved with other output operations.

## 5.2   Interaction

In pure functional languages, the handling of input and output does not require any extra language features. The input is treated as a list of characters just like any other, and the output is defined as a function of the input. However, there are extra programming techniques which need to be developed in the case of interactive programs.

For an interactive program, the main input is a stream of characters coming from the keyboard, and the main output is a stream of characters sent to the screen. These input and output streams must be interleaved, e.g. questions and answers must follow each other in the right order.

Operating systems normally provide two different methods of interaction which affect this interleaving – line interaction and character interaction. With line interaction, the input is typed in a line at a time, each line representing a command to which the program responds. With character interaction, which is more suitable for graphics programs for example, each character is a command which evokes an immediate response from the program. These two styles of interaction are described below.

A further issue which arises is that of storing global data which changes as questions are answered or commands given. Such global data is called the state of the program, and techniques for handling it are also described below.

### 5.2.1   Line Interaction

With **line interaction**, the keyboard input is passed one line at a time to the program. While a line is being typed in, the operating system is responsible for echoing the characters on the screen, and for allowing the user to edit the line using a DELETE or BACKSPACE key. Only when the user finally presses the RETURN or ENTER key is the final version of the line sent to the program by the operating system.

Line interaction is usually the default style of interaction, so no special action needs to be taken by the program. This style of interaction is very convenient because the program need not be concerned with echoing and line editing, and the processing of lines from the keyboard can be handled in a very similar way to the processing of lines from a file. In either case, the text appears to the program as a stream of characters. The only difference is the question of the correct interleaving of the input and output.

If there are no prompts involved, then writing a program using line interaction is quite simple. Although the input is passed to the program one

line at a time, the input still appears as a stream of characters $- to the
programmer, so the standard function *lines* is used to split $- into a list
of lines. This list is processed in some way to produce a list of output lines,
and these can be displayed using the standard function *lay* which attaches
a newline to the end of each line and then concatenates the lines into a single
stream. For example, a program which responds to each line typed in by
printing it out again in reverse can be accomplished by evaluating a one-line
expression:

```
?  lay [reverse l | l <- lines $-]
Line one
eno eniL
Line two
owt eniL
...
```

This interaction continues until the end-of-input convention is used to terminate the keyboard input, or until the program is interrupted.

To make the interleaving work properly in such programs, it is only
necessary to ensure that the function which is applied to the input lines in
order to produce the output lines, e.g. the list comprehension in the above
example, is a suitable stream function, as discussed in Section 3.2.2, so that
lines of output are produced at the same time as lines of input are being
read in.

The inclusion of prompts complicates the issue a little. A common mistake is to attempt to attach a prompt to each command-response pair:

```
?  lay ["> " ++ reverse l | l <- lines $-]      || WRONG
```

However, this results in the prompts appearing after each line has been typed
in rather than before. This mistake is not confined to functional languages
– it is also present in the following incorrect procedural code, because the
end-of-input test causes each command to be read in unexpectedly early:

```
while not end-of-input begin
    print prompt;
    read command;
    print response;
end
```

A little thought or experimentation reveals that there should be one
more prompt than there are commands and responses, and that the first

prompt should appear even if no commands are typed in at all. A correct
version of the line-reversal example is:

```
? "> " ++ concat [reverse l ++ "\n> " | l <- lines $-]
> Line one
eno eniL
> Line two
owt eniL
> ...
```

The initial prompt is output straight away, and subsequently each response
has a newline and a prompt attached to the end of it. The program can be
terminated with the usual end-of-input convention.

### 5.2.2   Character Interaction

With **character interaction**, each character typed at the keyboard is sent
straight to the program, and it is the program that is responsible for any
echoing or editing required. This style of interaction is suitable for programs
such as screen editors or graphics programs, which typically have single
character commands requiring immediate response.

Since line interaction is usually the default, some special operating system feature must be used to arrange for character interaction. Let us suppose that there is an operating system command *off* which enters character
interaction mode by switching off editing and echoing, and a command *on*
which reverses this.

A program using character interaction can then return as its result a
list of system messages which switch echoing off, send the output to the
screen, and then switch echoing on again. For example, the following program, which is started by evaluating *run*, echoes the numerical code of
each character typed by the user. Typing the character '*q*' terminates the
program:

```
run    =  [System "off", Stdout output, System "on"]
output =  lay [show (code c) | c <- input]
input  =  takewhile (~='q') $-
```

Here, *System* is a Miranda system message which sends a command to
the operating system for execution. There are no standards for character
interaction in operating systems. The actual commands for switching editing and echoing on and off vary, and indeed some operating systems do not

provide commands for it at all, but only procedure calls. Also, switching editing and echoing off may disable the ability to use the operating system's interruption and end-of-input conventions. This may make it difficult to terminate the program – hence the careful provision of a terminating character in the above example program.

To make character interaction facilities less dependent on the operating system, it would be better if they were built into the language. Newer functional languages such as Haskell (see Chapter 9) do just this and it is also planned to add such facilities to Miranda.

A further complication is access to screen or graphics facilities. It is often possible to place text at arbitrary positions on the screen by including control characters in the output stream – such facilities are often used by programs which involve text editing. Unfortunately, there is at present no widely used standard for such use of control characters – rather each kind of terminal or screen has its own conventions.

Similarly, graphics facilities are not well standardised, and they are usually provided in the form of procedure libraries, making them difficult to use from functional languages. With current functional languages, most of which do not have built-in graphics facilities, often the best that can be done is to arrange for the standard output from a functional program to be fed into a separate procedural program which interprets the stream of characters as graphics commands. Considerable effort is currently being put into standardising graphics and windowing systems, and this is likely to help to make graphics interfaces to functional languages more widespread in the future.

### 5.2.3   State

A program often needs to store global data which gets updated as the program proceeds. This global data is called the **state** of the program. Functional languages have no explicit notion of state or of updating, so how can such programs be written?

The answer lies in the discussion of loop design in Section 3.2.1. A loop function has arguments which represent the essential values which vary as the loop proceeds. Program design often benefits from the same kind of analysis on a larger scale. The first thing to do is to work out the essential information which must be stored in order to represent the current state of the program at any stage, and then decide how it changes. The overall structure of the program can then be represented as a loop function, with the state being held in its arguments.

A useful loop function in this context is the standard function *scan*. The *scan* function takes three arguments, which are the same as those of the standard function *foldl*. The *scan* function returns a list containing the result of applying *foldl* to each initial sublist of the third argument in turn. For example, a list of running totals can be produced by:

```
?  scan (+) 0 [1..5]
[0,1,3,6,10,15]
```

In the context of an interactive program with a state, the first argument can be thought of as a *do* function which takes a current state and a command and returns a new state. The second argument acts as an initial state, and the third is a list of commands. The commands are obeyed in turn using the *do* function and the list of states produced is returned.

The above example can be converted into a complete interactive program which keeps track of a running total, and repeatedly prompts for a command consisting of a number to be added into the total with the + operator. It is convenient to represent the state as a pair consisting of the running total and the current message to be displayed:

```
run   =  concat [snd s ++ "\nNext: " | s <- states]
states  =  scan do start $+
start  =  (0,"Please type in numbers.")
do (n,cs) m  =  (n+m, "Total is " ++ show (n+m))
```

The program is started by typing *run*. The symbol *$+* is used to read in a stream of numbers, and *scan* is used to form a stream of states. The messages are extracted from the states and concatenated, with newlines and prompts added, to form the output. The *do* function takes a current state and a number, and produces a new state by updating the running total and replacing the output message.

Many interactive programs have the same overall form, and the same technique can be used to control the interaction with the user, as with the first two example programs below.

## 5.3   A Personal Notebook Program

Some of the details about input, output, interaction and state which have been discussed above can now be put into practice in a slightly more realistic example program. The program is one which allows a text file to be used as a personal notebook, such as a diary or an address book. If used as a diary, for example, each entry could contain a date and a reminder of something to be done. The program could be used to add and remove entries from the diary, or to find all the entries containing a given date, and so list all the things to be done on that day.

The notebook is kept in a text file, with one entry on each line. The program reads the data in from the file, allows you to consult and update it, and then writes the final version of the data back into the file when you quit. There are commands to add a new entry, to find all the entries containing a given string, and to delete all the entries containing a given string.

The program consists of two separate modules. The first deals with interaction with the user and the overall logic of the program. The second defines the representation of the state and operations as abstract data types.

## 5.3.1 The Interaction Module

The program is started by typing *run*. This returns a list containing two system messages: a *Stdout* message which sends the program's prompts and responses to the screen, and a *Tofile* message which writes out the final version of the notebook file. The initial contents of the file are read in using the standard *read* function, and the final contents are extracted from the final state.

```
run    =  [Stdout out, seq get (Tofile "notes" put)]
get    =  read "notes"
put    =  extract (last states)
out    =  concat [output s | s <- states]
states =  takeuntil end (scan do (new get) $+)
```

The standard function *seq* is used to ensure that the *read* is started before the *Tofile*. Without this precaution, if you were to quit the program immediately without giving any commands, the *Tofile* message would cause the notebook file to be opened for writing, destroying its contents, before being opened for reading.

Each state contains the current contents of the notebook and a current message to be displayed to the user. The state module provides functions *new* to create an initial state, *do* to apply an operation to the current state to form a new state, *output* to get the user message from a state, *end* to detect the final state, and *extract* to convert a state back to text.

A stream of commands is read from the user using the standard *$+* symbol. The standard *scan* function uses these commands as state operations to form a stream of states, and a function *takeuntil* is used to stop when the final state is reached. The *takeuntil* function, like *takewhile*, returns the initial portion of a list. It uses a test function to determine the last member of the list to return and is defined by:

```
takeuntil f []  =  []
takeuntil f (x:rxs)
=  [x],                      if f x
=  x : takeuntil f rxs,   otherwise
```

This function is used in preference to *takewhile* because *takewhile* examines the member of a list beyond the last one it returns. In the current interactive setting, this would force the program to read in one more command after the final state.

### 5.3.2  The State Module

The second module defines the way in which the current state of the program, and the operations on it, are represented. It is convenient in programs of this kind to treat the state and operations as abstract types to ensure a clean division between modules. The state type and the operation type are closely linked, and so must be declared in a single **abstype** declaration:

```
abstype   state, operation  with
    new  ::   text->state
    output  ::   state->text
    end  ::   state->bool
    do  ::   state->operation->state
    extract  ::   state->text

    enter  ::   [char]->operation
    find  ::   [char]->operation
    delete  ::   [char]->operation
    quit  ::   operation
```

These type declarations are sufficient to ensure that the type of the values read in by *$+* in the interaction module can be determined by the compiler.

The state is represented as a triple containing the notebook data stored as a list of lines, a current message to be displayed on the screen, and a boolean indicating whether the state is the final one. We have chosen to represent an operation as a function which takes one state to the next:

```
state   ==   ([text],text,bool)
operation
==   ([text],text,bool)->([text],text,bool)
text   ==   [char]


new cs  =   (lines cs,  help,  False)
help  =  "Commands: enter, find, delete, quit\n> "
output (db,cs,b)  =   cs
end (db,cs,b)  =  b
do state op  =   op state
extract (db,cs,b)  =   lay db
```

The commands which the user can type in are defined as operations which convert the current state into the next one:

```
enter l (db,cs,b)  =   (db++[l], "OK\n> ", b)


find s (db,cs,b)
=   (db, "Nothing found.\n> ", b),  if entries = []
=   (db, lay entries ++ "> ", b),  otherwise
    where
    entries  =  [l | l<-db; substring s l]


delete s (db,cs,b)
=   ([l | l<-db; ~ substring s l], "OK\n> ", b)


quit (db,cs,b)  =   (db,"Notebook stored\n",True)
```

The user types in a call to one of these functions, omitting the last argument which represents the current state. For example:

```
> find "friday"
```

This makes use of the partial application feature described in Section 2.4.4. A command is a partial application, i.e. a function which is "waiting" for its last argument. Thus every command has the type *state->state*, and is applied to the current state by the *do* function above.

To complete the personal notebook program, the function *substring* which tests whether a string *s* is a substring of a line *l* is defined by:

```
substring s l
=  or [s = take (#s) (drop n l) | n <- [0..#l-#s]]
```

## 5.4    A Telephone Exchange Program

This section illustrates the way in which a functional program can be used
both as a specification for some large project, and also as a prototype implementation. The final version of such a project might be written in a
procedural language, or implemented in hardware.

The specification of a project needs to be very precise, so that every-
one involved in the project can agree on exactly what is required, and so
that the specification can be discussed and investigated before any implementation effort is expended. Such project specifications are often carried
out using special purpose, mathematically based languages such as VDM or
Z (see Jones [7] or Spivey [14]) which have features allowing powerful self-
consistency checks to be made on the specification. Functional languages
have a great deal in common with such specification languages, sharing the
same economical high-level style and sound mathematical basis, and can be
used instead of them, or alongside them. This section illustrates how some
of the consistency checks which specification languages provide can be built
into functional programs.

A specification of the kind described here can also be used as a prototype
implementation to demonstrate to potential users the approach being taken,
to investigate its suitability, and to develop and adapt it with a minimum
of re-programming effort. Such a combined specification and prototype is
called an **animation**, or an **executable specification**. Since functional
languages are complete programming languages, they are very suitable for
producing such animations, particularly if general purpose high-level modules such as those of Chapter 4 are used.

In this section, we produce an extremely simple animation of a telephone
exchange, i.e. a system which connects a group of telephones together and
provides the necessary facilities for making calls. The overall structure of the
program is very similar to the personal notebook program in the previous
section. The interaction module uses the `takeuntil` function defined in
Section 5.3.2 and consists of the two definitions:

```
run    =  concat [output s | s <- states]
states  =  takeuntil end (scan do new $+)
```

The interface to the state and operation module uses the set module
described in Section 4.4 and includes state functions as in the notebook
program, and three operations:

```
%include "sets"
```

```
abstype   state,   operation   with
   new         ::    state
   output      ::    state->[char]
   end         ::    state->bool
   do          ::    state->operation->state

   call        ::    phone->phone->operation
   hangup      ::    phone->operation
   quit        ::    operation
```

The representation of the state consists of an exchange, a user message and an indication of the final state. An operation is a state transformer, as before. An exchange consists of a set of conversations, and a conversation involves a set of phones. A phone is represented by its number, of type *[char]* rather than *num* since phone numbers may include leading zeros:

```
state   ==   (exchange,[char],bool)
operation
==   (exchange,[char],bool)->(exchange,[char],bool)
exchange   ==   set conversation
conversation   ==   set phone
phone   ==   [char]

new   =   (emptyset,help,False)
help   =   "Commands: call m n, hangup n, quit\n> "
output (ex,cs,b)   =   cs
end (ex,cs,b)   =   b
do state op   =   op state
```

The operations allow us to illustrate the ideas of preconditions and invariants, which can be added to any animation as consistency checks, and refinement – the process of moving towards a full implementation in stages.

## 5.4.1   Preconditions

In formal specifications a precondition is added to each operation. A **precondition** is a check that the arguments of the operation are sensible, so that it is meaningful for the operation to go ahead.

The operations provided for the telephone exchange are as follows. The operation *call p1 p2* sets up a call between two given phones. The precondition is a boolean value *pre* which specifies that a phone cannot call itself, and that neither of the two phones must be engaged in a conversation already. The operation then passes the current state, the precondition, and an updated state in which the new conversation is added, to a support function *process* described below. The operation *hangup p* which shuts down the conversation in which the phone *p* is involved is defined similarly:

```
call p1 p2 (ex,cs,b)
=  process (ex,cs,b) pre (ex',cs',b)  where
     pre  =  p1 ~= p2 & ~ in busy p1 & ~ in busy p2
     busy =  setof [p | c <- list ex; p <- list c]
     ex'  =  insert ex (setof [p1,p2])
     cs'  =  show [list c | c <- list ex'] ++ "\n> "


hangup p (ex,cs,b)
=  process (ex,cs,b) pre (ex',cs',b)  where
     pre  =  or [in c p | c <- list ex]
     ex'  =  difference ex (setof [conv])
     conv =  the [c | c <- list ex; in c p]
     the [x]  = x
     cs'  =  show [list c | c <- list ex'] ++ "\n> "


quit (ex,cs,b)  =  (ex,"",True)
```

The definition of *hangup* depends on the laziness feature of Miranda in a minor way. If the precondition of the operation fails, then evaluation of the updated state using the function *the* would cause an error. However, the *process* function is defined in such a way that if the precondition fails, the new state is not evaluated and so the error does not occur.

## 5.4.2   Invariants

An **invariant** captures conventions and properties which a data type has, but which cannot be specified using the type system. An invariant can be represented as a function which tests a value and returns a boolean indicating whether the value has the right properties. In the case of the telephone exchange, the invariant specifies that each conversation currently taking place in an exchange involves exactly two phones, and that a phone cannot take part in more than one conversation at once:

```
inv ex
=  and [# list c = 2 | c <- list ex] &
     and [disjoint c1 c2 | c1,c2 <- list ex; c1~=c2]
```

The invariant provides a powerful consistency check on the animation because it represents a static view of what is possible, while the operations form a dynamic view of what is possible. These two views should agree, in the sense that any state which can be produced from the initial state by using the operations should satisfy the invariant, and any state which satisfies the invariant should be capable of being produced by a suitable sequence of operations. This consistency property can, in principle, be checked by formal mathematical proof.

The invariant can be used as a practical tool by testing that it is still satisfied every time the state is updated during use of the animation. It is usually too expensive to include such invariant checking in the final implementation, but if it can be proved, or at least demonstrated beyond reasonable doubt, that the operations preserve the invariant, then the invariant is guaranteed to hold, and need not be checked in the implementation.

The support function *process* checks that the precondition of an operation succeeds, and the new updated state satisfies the invariant. If not, it returns a suitable message and leaves the exchange unaltered. Of course, if the animation is correct, then the invariant should never be violated:

```
process (ex,cs,b) pre (ex',cs',b')
=   (ex,"Precondition failed\n> ",b),   if ~pre
=   (ex,"Invariant violated\n> ",b),    if ~inv ex'
=   (ex',cs',b'),                       otherwise
```

Precondition checks should normally be left in the implementation, unless it can be shown that an operation is only ever called in situations in which its precondition is true.

The animation of the telephone exchange is now complete, and an example of its use is:

```
?  run
Commands: call m n, hangup n, quit
> call "123" "456"
[["123","456"]]
> call "321" "456"
Precondition failed                    (456 is engaged)
> call "321" "999"
[["123","456"],["321","999"]]
> hangup "123"
[["321","999"]]
> quit
```

### 5.4.3   Refinement

The process of **refinement** involves producing more detailed prototypes, each derived from the previous one, culminating in a full implementation. Each step either adds more features to the system, or implements existing features in a more efficient way. Each version acts as a specification for the next refinement, and it is possible to prove or demonstrate that a refinement correctly implements its specification.

In the case of the telephone exchange, a more detailed prototype can be written in Miranda to incorporate dialling conventions on the individual phones. We give a brief description of the refinement here, and leave it to the reader to complete – see the exercises.

The *call* operation is replaced by operations *pickup p* to pick up a phone, *putdown p* to put down a phone, and *press p d* to simulate the pressing of a digit on a phone. A further operation *install p* is added so that only installed phones can call or be called. At the same time, the representation of the exchange is changed to be closer to the final implementation. It is represented as a table with an entry for each phone giving its current status. The status is represented by the type:

```
status
::=  Free | Dialling_tone | Dialling no |
     Ringing_tone no | Ringing no | Talking no |
     Engaged_tone | Unobtainable_tone
no   ==   [char]
```

The invariant specifies that no installed phone number is a prefix of any other, that if the status of a phone is *Dialling n* then the number *n* dialled so far is a valid prefix of an installed phone number, and that in the cases *Ringing_tone*, *Ringing* and *Talking*, the associated number is that of another installed phone with a corresponding status. As before, the invariant provides a powerful consistency check – a state should satisfy the invariant if and only if it can be generated from the initial state using the operations provided.

The correspondence between a refinement and its specification can be made precise by defining a **retrieve** function, that is a function from the state of the refinement to the state of the specification. In the case of the telephone exchange, this is a function from a status table to a set of pairs of phones. The function extracts from the table those pairs of phones which are currently talking to each other.

The refinement can then be shown to implement its specification correctly by showing that the new operations do to the new state what the old operations do to the old state. In the case of the telephone exchange, the refinement has a lot more detail in it, so that for most operations on the refined state, the equivalent on the old state is to have no effect. However, picking up a ringing phone, and putting down a talking one, have exactly the same effect as the original *call* and *hangup* operations.

## 5.5  An Expert System

The final example program in the chapter is a simple expert system which illustrates some more advanced programming techniques. An expert system is a program which solves problems in some restricted area of human knowledge. It consists of a **knowledge base**, i.e. a collection of rules about the chosen subject area, and a **shell**, i.e. a general purpose program which makes logical deductions from the knowledge base and which interacts with the user. For example, in an expert system for recognising animals, the knowledge base might contain the statements:

```
X is a zebra if X has stripes and X has hooves
X is a tiger if X has stripes and X has claws
```

The shell is used to interact with the user, by asking questions to which the user gives *yes* or *no* answers, and suggesting solutions:

```
?   run
Solving: the animal is X
Is it true that the animal has stripes?
yes
Is it true that the animal has hooves?
no
Is it true that the animal has claws?
yes
Solution: X = a tiger. More?
no
```

The program described here is a prototype expert system which can be used for demonstration purposes. Many of the features which would be needed for a full scale expert system are omitted, but the program includes those features of expert systems which pose the most interesting programming problems. Expert systems are more commonly written using logic programming languages, which have built-in facilities for knowledge representation and logical deduction, and you should consult a book on logic programming (e.g. Sterling & Shapiro [15]) to find out more about them.

The program consists of several modules, presented here in such a way that each depends on the preceding ones. First, there is a knowledge module which provides a language in which knowledge is represented. Second, there is a matching module providing an algorithm for an extended form of matching called unification. This is needed for comparing goals to be solved against the information in the knowledge base. Third, there is a searching module which provides the searching and backtracking facilities which are needed in order to make deductions from the rules in the knowledge base. Finally, there is an interaction module which deals with asking questions and getting answers from the user, and presenting solutions to problems.

## 5.5.1   The Knowledge Module

The knowledge base itself is represented by a file containing the rules about the chosen subject area. To continue with the rather rudimentary example of animal recognition, which the reader is left to complete, the knowledge base might be stored in a text file called *animals* in which each rule is represented as a line of text. Each line is a sequence of words without punctuation, and each word is in lower case, except for variables such as *X* which begin with capitals:

```
X is a dog if mammal describes X and X can bark
mammal describes X if X has hair or X has milk
```

A module is needed to read in the knowledge base and transform the rules into an internal data structure. This module uses the table module described in Section 4.6, and exports the table facilities along with its own for use by the other modules:

```
%include "tables"
%export "tables" expr showexpr vars rules problem
```

To make the language as flexible and uniform as possible, rules are represented internally as expression trees using the type *expr*. This is very similar to the type *tree* defined in Section 4.5, with strings as labels, except that it is convenient to distinguish the variables. The *showexpr* function displays expressions as text. It assumes that there are only variables, constants and infix operators, and that no parentheses are necessary. The *vars* function returns a list of the variables which appear in an expression:

```
expr  ::=  Expr [char] [expr] | Var [char]

showexpr (Var x)  =  x
showexpr (Expr x [])  =  x
showexpr (Expr op [e1,e2])
=  showexpr e1 ++ " " ++ op ++ " " ++ showexpr e2

vars e
= mkset (vlist e)  where
    vlist (Var x)  =  [Var x]
    vlist (Expr x es)  =  concat [vlist e | e <- es]
```

As an example, the statement *"X has teeth"* is represented by the expression tree *Expr "has" [Var "X", Expr "teeth" []]*. The type *expr* is not made into an abstract data type, since it is convenient to be able to use pattern matching on it.

The functions *rule*, *goal*, *relation* and *noun* are used to translate the rules in the knowledge base from lines of text into expression trees. They specify that a rule is of the form *r if g* for some relation *r* and goal *g*, that a compound goal is built up from subgoals using *or* and *and*, that a simple goal is a relation, and that a relation is of the form *n1 op n2* for nouns *n1* and *n2*, and infix verb *op*:

```
rule ws  =  split ws relation "if" goal

goal ws
= split ws goal "or" goal,   if member ws "or"
= split ws goal "and" goal,  if member ws "and"
= relation ws,               otherwise

relation ws
= split ws noun op noun  where
    op  =  hd [w | w<-ws; member verbs w]
    verbs  =  ["is","has","can","eats","describes"]

noun [a,x]
=  noun [a++" "++x],   member ["a","an","the"] a
noun [x]  =  Var x,  if 'A' <= hd x <= 'Z'
noun [x]  =  Expr x []
```

The ordering of the tests in *goal* specifies that *and* binds tighter than *or*. For extra readability, an article *a*, *an* or *the* is treated as part of a noun.

The translation functions use the support function *split* which takes a list of words, searches for a given operator (verb), and uses it as the label of an expression tree. The words to the left and to the right of the operator are translated into subtrees using given translation functions. The *words* function divides a line of text up into words:

```
split ws f op g
=   Expr op [f lhs, g rhs]
    where
    lhs  =  takewhile (~=op) ws
    rhs  =  tl (dropwhile (~=op) ws)

words []  =  []
words (' ':rcs)  =  words rcs
words cs
=   takewhile (~=' ') cs :
    words (dropwhile (~=' ') cs)
```

Although the language defined by these translation functions is quite readable, it is a very restricted and stylised one. Moreover, the functions contain no error checking, and so the knowledge base must be constructed and tested with care. However, the program is designed so that the user is never required to write statements in this language, only to give *yes* or *no* answers to questions. The functions described so far are rather crude examples of parsing functions, as described in Section 6.1.

The knowledge module provides a function *rules* which returns those rules in the knowledge base which are relevant to a given relation, i.e. those for which the relation to the left of the *"if"* has the same verb. This is done by creating a table called *definitions* with an entry for each verb:

```
rules (Expr v ns)  =  lookup definitions v []

definitions
=   tableof [(v, def v) | v<-verbs]  where
    def v  =  [r | r<-rs; verb r = v]
    verbs  =  mkset [verb r | r <- rs]
    verb (Expr "if" [Expr v ns, g])  =  v
    rs  =  [rule (words l) | l <- ls]
    ls  =  lines (read "animals")
```

If the knowledge base contains rules relevant to a particular kind of relation, e.g. *the animal is X*, then those rules are taken to form the complete definition of that relation. If there are no relevant rules, e.g. for *the animal has stripes*, then its truth is determined by asking the user.

Finally, the module provides an initial goal which describes the kind of problem which the expert system is designed to solve:

> *problem   =   goal (words "the animal is X")*

In a full expert system implementation, the language in which knowledge is represented is usually more extensive, allowing for parentheses, operators with various precedences, relations with varying numbers of arguments, data structures in place of simple nouns, and negative information. Some expert systems also have a means of dealing with uncertain information by specifying measures of confidence.

Building an effective expert system requires the difficult skill of **knowledge engineering**, that is the ability to extract the information and the judgements which human experts in the subject unconsciously use in making decisions, and to represent this knowledge as a coherent and self-consistent collection of precise rules.

## 5.5.2   The Matching Module

In an expert system, goals need to be matched against the left hand sides of rules in order to make deductions. This matching is rather like pattern matching (see Section 2.4), except that instead of a value being matched against a pattern, two patterns are matched against each other. In other words, two expressions are compared, both of which may contain variables. The matching module provides facilities for doing this, importing and passing on the facilities from the *knowledge* module:

> *%include "knowledge"*
> *%export "knowledge" env subst fail ok match*

Information is gained about variables during the matching process. For example, if the relation *X eats Y* is matched against *Z eats leaves* then *X* must be equal to *Z*, and *Y* must stand for *leaves*. This information could be represented by recording the most up-to-date expression currently known for each variable in a table called an **environment**, as shown on the left. If *Z* was subsequently discovered to stand for *a zebra*, then the table would be updated as on the right:

| | |
|---|---|
| *(X, Z)* | *(X, a zebra)* |
| *(Y, leaves)* | *(Y, leaves)* |
| *(Z, Z)* | *(Z, a zebra)* |

The trouble with keeping the most up-to-date expression for each variable in the environment is that each time an entry is made, as with Z = a zebra above, all the other entries need to be checked to see if they contain references to Z which need updating.

An alternative approach is to keep a minimum of information in the environment. If nothing is known about a variable, then no entry is stored for it. When an entry is made, the other entries are not brought up to date. The above example would then produce the tables:

```
(X,  Z)                              (X,  Z)
(Y,  leaves)                         (Y,  leaves)
                                     (Z,  a zebra)
```

With these conventions, an environment can be updated using the normal *update* function from the table module. However, when an entry is looked up, the expression returned may need further processing. For example, in the table on the right above, looking up X returns Z, which needs to be looked up again to return *a zebra*. To deal with this problem in as general a way as possible, a substitution function *subst* is provided which translates a given expression into its most up-to-date form by replacing the variables in it recursively:

```
env   ==   table expr expr

subst t (Expr x es)  =  Expr x [subst t e | e<-es]
subst t (Var x)
=   e,            if e = Var x
=   subst t e,    otherwise
    where
    e  =  lookup t (Var x) (Var x)
```

If the expression is a compound one, substitution is performed on each subexpression. If it is a variable, then it is looked up in the environment. If nothing is known about the variable, i.e. there is no entry for it so that the default (the variable itself) is returned, then the variable is left unchanged. Otherwise *subst* is called recursively on the result.

In cases where a problem may have no solution or many solutions, it is convenient to return the solutions in a list. In line with this convention, if the *match* function below fails it returns the empty list, and if it succeeds it returns a list with one member. To make the definition of *match* more readable, we define:

```
fail  =  []
ok x  =  [x]
```

The *match* function is used to match two expressions, and is called recursively on corresponding pairs of subexpressions. It implements the well-known **unification** algorithm used in the implementation of logic programming languages. If a call to *match* succeeds, the result is an updated environment containing the extra information gained about the variables in order to make the subexpressions match.

The *match* function has two arguments. The first is the result of matching previous pairs of subexpressions, and the second is the the current pair of subexpressions:

```
match [] (e1,e2)  =  fail
match [t] (e1,e2)
=  compare t (subst t e1) (subst t e2)

compare t (Expr x1 es1) (Expr x2 es2)
=  foldl match (ok t) (zip2 es1 es2),  if x1 = x2
=  fail,                               otherwise
compare t (Var x) (Var y)
=  ok (update t (Var x) (Var y)),  if x ~= y
=  ok t,                           otherwise
compare t (Var x) e
=  ok (update t (Var x) e),  if ~ occurs (Var x) e
=  fail,                     otherwise
compare t e (Var x)
=  compare t (Var x) e

occurs v (Expr x es)  =  or [occurs v e | e<-es]
occurs v (Var x)      =  Var x = v
```

First, *subst* is used on the two expressions to bring them up to date according to the information gleaned from previous matches. Then the resulting expressions are compared. If they are compound expression trees with the same root, then the standard function *foldl* is used to match up corresponding pairs of subexpressions, the table being used to accumulate information about variables. If either of the expressions is a variable, and they are not equal, then a suitable entry is made in the table. Before making an entry, a check is made to see that the variable does not occur in the expression being entered for it, since this would represent an impossible equation (e.g. $X = not\ X$).

In implementations of logic programming languages, in which unification is carried out very frequently, the algorithm is made more efficient by omitting the *occurs* check (which fails quite infrequently) and by only performing partial substitution in the initial call to *compare* – it is sufficient to make sure that the roots of the expression trees are up-to-date, since the subtrees will get substituted anyway later in the algorithm.

### 5.5.3   The Searching Module

The next module deals with searching for solutions to problems. It works by making logical deductions (also called inferences), and is often called an **inference engine**. It uses "backwards" or goal-directed inference. The value of *problem* from the knowledge module is the initial goal. Compound goals are reduced to simple goals, and simple goals are either matched against rules in the knowledge base, or are presented as questions to the user.

The module imports the matching module, and re-exports it, along with the type *result* and the function *solve*, for use by the interaction module. The module also requires a table *info* of information provided by the interaction module. As explained in Section 4.1.3, modules cannot be directly mutually recursive, and must be capable of being compiled in a particular order. To allow the searching module to be compiled before the interaction module, *info* is defined as a free parameter:

```
%include "match"
%export "match" result solve
%free info :: table expr bool;
```

A result of a search is either a solution to the goal, or a question to ask the user. A solution is represented as an environment containing the values which have been determined for the variables, together with a list of fresh variable names which are guaranteed not to clash with any already in the environment. These names are used when a solution to one subgoal is used as a starting point to generate solutions to another subgoal. A question is represented as an expression containing no variables:

```
result   ::=   Soln env [expr] | Question expr
```

The function which searches for solutions to a goal is called *solve*. It returns a list of results, i.e. a mixture of solutions and questions. The first

argument to *solve* is the result obtained so far, and the second is the goal
which remains to be solved:

```
solve (Question q) g  =  [Question q]

solve soln (Expr "or" [g1,g2])
=  solve soln g1 ++ solve soln g2

solve soln (Expr "and" [g1,g2])
=  concat [solve res g2 | res <- solve soln g1]

solve soln g
=  find soln g rs,   if rs ~= []
=  ask soln g,        otherwise
   where
   rs  =  rules g
```

The first equation ensures that questions needed to solve subgoals are returned as questions needed to solve the main goal. For a compound goal *g1*
*or g2* the results for *g1* are followed by the results for *g2*. For *g1 and g2*,
each result for *g1* is used as a starting point to search for results to *g2*, and
the lists of results generated are concatenated to form a single list.

To solve a simple goal, the relevant rules are extracted from the knowledge base and *find* is used to generate new goals. If there are no relevant
rules, then *ask* is used to ask the user:

```
find soln g rs
=  concat [try soln' g r' | (soln',r') <- copies]
   where
   copies  =  [copy soln r | r<-rs]

try (Soln t vs) g (Expr "if" [e1,e2])
=  solve (Soln (hd m) vs) e2,   if m ~= fail
=  [],                           otherwise
   where
   m  =  match (ok t) (g,e1)

copy (Soln t vs) e
=  ((Soln t (drop (#xs) vs)), subst tab e)   where
   tab  =  tableof (zip2 xs (take (#xs) vs))
   xs   =  vars e
```

```
ask (Soln t vs) g
=   Question (subst t g) : soln  where
    soln
    =  ok (Soln t vs),   if ans = True
    =  fail,             otherwise
    ans  =  lookup info (subst t g) undef
```

In *find*, a fresh copy is created of each relevant rule so that the variables in
the rule do not clash with any already being used. Then the function *try*
is used to test each rule. If the rule is *e1 if e2*, then the current goal *g* is
matched with *e1*. If the match succeeds, then the resulting environment is
used to search for solutions to the new goal *e2*.

The function *ask* solves a goal by returning a question to ask the user,
and then looking up the answer in a table called *info* containing an entry
for each question which the user is asked. This table is guaranteed to have
the required answer in it, so the default argument to *lookup* is *undef* – a
standard value which produces a program error with a suitable message. It is
assumed that by the time a goal is processed by *ask*, all the variables have
known values, i.e. the question *subst t g* contains no variables, though
there is no explicit check for this.

The *ask* function, and thus the *solve* function, is a function taking
the user's answers as input (in the form of the *info* table) and returning
the questions to ask the user as output (embedded in the list of results),
as described in Section 1.3.2. Care has to be taken over the interactive
behaviour of *ask*. In particular, it returns the question before evaluating
*soln*, which involves processing the answer.

Many other search problems can also be solved using the list-of-solutions
method which avoids the explicit backtracking which would be needed in a
procedural language – see the exercises for examples. Laziness ensures that
if only the first solution to a problem is needed, then only as much work
is done as is necessary to produce that solution. If the second solution is
subsequently needed, then the search will be continued where it was left off.

### 5.5.4   The Interaction Module

The interaction module is the main one which controls the entire program.
It uses the facilities provided by all the previous modules. It also supplies
the info table used by the search module, so its interface is:

```
%include "search" info = info;
```

The program as a whole is started by typing *run*. This prints out the overall problem being solved, and then displays the solutions and questions returned from a call to *solve*:

```
run
=   "Solving: " ++ showexpr problem ++ "\n" ++
    display results replies
```

The list of results is obtained by calling *solve* on the value of *problem*, which is provided by the knowledge module, in the context of an empty environment and (infinite) list of fresh variable names given by *newsoln*. This list of results is then filtered by the *strip* function to avoid asking the same question twice. The first argument to *strip* is a list of the questions asked so far, and the second is the list of remaining results. The *strip* function has to be carefully designed as a stream function to ensure that it has the right interactive properties:

```
results
=   strip [] (solve newsoln problem)   where
    strip qs []   =   []
    strip qs (Question q : rs)
        =   strip qs rs,                    if member qs q
        =   Question q : strip (q:qs) rs,   otherwise
    strip qs (soln:rs)   =   soln : strip qs rs

newsoln
=   Soln (tableof []) [Var ('X': show n) | n<-[0..]]
```

Each solution or question in the list *results* causes an reply to be read in from the user. In the case of a solution to the problem, the values determined for the variables are displayed, and the user is asked if any more solutions are required. In the case of a question, the question is displayed and an answer read in. The list of replies is defined using the identifier *replies* for which a type declaration is given so that the compiler can determine the type of *$+*. The identifiers *yes* and *no* are defined so that the user can type them in as replies:

```
replies :: [bool]
replies   =   $+
yes   =   True
no   =   False
```

To form the table *info* of information provided by the user, the results
and replies are paired up, then the pairs involving a question and answer
are filtered out and turned into a table. The table must be a lazy one, as
described in Section 4.6 – the pairs must not be evaluated until needed by
*solve* so that no answer is read in until the corresponding question has
been asked:

```
info
=   lazy_tableof [(q,a) | (Question q, a) <- pairs]
    where
    pairs  =  zip2 results replies
```

Finally, the *display* function displays the list of results. It takes the
replies as a second argument to work out when to stop – which is when there
are no more replies (the user has typed the end-of-input character) or the
user replies *no* when asked if more solutions are required. Again, care has
to be taken over laziness here – the text to be printed for a result must be
returned before the list of remaining replies is evaluated:

```
display [] as  =  "No (more) solutions\n"
display (Question q : rs) as
=   "Is it true that " ++ showexpr q ++ "?\n" ++
    display rs (tl as)
display (Soln t vs : rs) as
=   "Solution: " ++ sol ++ ". More?\n" ++ etc   where
    sol  =  showvars t (vars problem)
    etc
    =   "",                       if as=[] \/ hd as = False
    =   display rs (tl as),  otherwise

showvars t vs
=   foldr1 join (map printvar vs)   where
    join x y  =  x ++ "; " ++ y
    printvar v
    =   showexpr v ++ " = " ++ showexpr (subst t v)
```

This prototype of an expert system leaves out many features which a
full implementation would have. Perhaps the most notable omission is the
ability to explain, on demand from the user, why a particular question is
being asked or how a particular solution was deduced. However, there is
no particular difficulty in adding such features. They involve extending the

*solve* function so that the rules which are currently being investigated are stored with each question, and the rules which have been successfully used are stored with each solution.

## 5.6 Exercises

1. Write a program which prints out the length of each line which the user types in.

2. Using the $+ symbol, write a program which acts as a calculator, repeatedly prompting for a numerical expression which it then evaluates.

3. Find out what commands your computer provides for character interaction, and what conventions your terminal or screen uses to allow the cursor to be moved around (e.g. use the program in Section 5.2.2 to find out what characters are generated by the cursor keys). Write a character interaction program which allows the user to move the cursor around with the cursor keys and to type characters anywhere on the screen.

4. Write a program which implements a personal telephone directory as follows. The directory should be stored permanently in a text file, each line consisting of a name and a telephone number. The file should be read in and converted into a table using the *tableof* function from the table module described in Section 4.6. Commands should be provided to add or update entries, and to look up existing entries. The final version of the table should be stored back in the file when the program terminates.

5. Complete the refinement of the telephone exchange program, as described in Section 5.4.3. Check, to your own satisfaction, that the refinement is self consistent by showing that any state which satisfies the invariant can be generated by a suitable sequence of operations, and that each operation preserves the invariant.

   Define the retrieve function which links the refinement to its specification by generating the original state corresponding to a given state in the refinement. Check that the refinement is a correct implementation of its specification by showing that the only operations which have any equivalent effect on the original state are picking up a ringing phone and putting down a talking one, and that the equivalent effect of these is the same as *call* and *hangup*.

6. Suppose you are given a list of numbers such as *[2, 3, 4, 5, 6]* and you need to split it into two sublists with equal sums (in this case, *[2, 3, 5]* and *[4, 6]*). Write a program to solve this problem using the list-of-solutions search technique described in Section 5.5.3, as follows. Define a function *search* which takes a list of numbers and a target number, and returns a list of all those sublists which add up to the target. The result list should consist of those solutions which include the first member of the original list, followed by those solutions which do not (thus involving two recursive calls to *search*).

7. Write a search program to solve the famous problem of placing 8 chess queens on a chess board so that no queen is attacking any other, i.e. placing 8 objects on an 8 by 8 grid so that no two are in line, horizontally or vertically or diagonally. Represent a position on the board as a pair *(x, y)* with *x* and *y* in the range 1 to 8. Define a function *inline* which takes two positions and returns a boolean indicating whether the positions are in line. Use this to define a function *extend* which takes a list of compatible positions (a partial solution) and returns a list of solutions with one more position added. Use this in turn to define a function *queens*, with one argument *n*, which returns the list of all solutions with *n* queens. The solution to the original problem is then *hd (queens 8)*. There are two ways to speed up the search. One is to note that there must be one queen in every row, so you only need search for solutions in which the first position has *x=1*, the second has *x=2* and so on. Also, there are few solutions with queens near the corners of the board, so you can let *y* run through *[4,5,3,6,2,7,1,8]*, say, rather than *[1..8]*.

# Chapter 6

# High Level Implementation

From this chapter onwards, we turn away from the art of programming, and concentrate on the internal features of functional languages – how they are implemented and how they are given a precise meaning.

Some knowledge of how programs are compiled and run is essential for experienced programmers who want to get the most out of a programming language. In this chapter and the next, we will give an outline description of the way in which functional languages are implemented, using Miranda as our example language.

Functional language compilers, as with compilers for other languages, are usually regarded as being in two parts. The first part, sometimes called the **front end**, deals with the high-level aspects of implementation, and is described in this chapter. The second part, the **back end**, deals with the low-level aspects of implementation, namely data representation and code generation, and is dealt with in the next chapter.

The front end can be thought of as a series of transformations, each of which changes the program by adding to it, simplifying it, or optimising it. For simplicity, the transformations will be described by giving examples of their effect, rather than by providing exact rules. Moreover, the interactions between the transformations will be ignored, and some issues such as the separate compilation of scripts and the reporting of errors will not be dealt with at all.

Many of the transformations described in this chapter can be thought of as **source to source** transformations, i.e. ones which convert a source program into another equivalent one. The final result of the front end can be regarded as a greatly altered program, which is nevertheless still equivalent to the original. The front end thus carries out high level processing which is independent of the details of the computer on which the program is being

129

compiled. The effects of each transformation will be described below, where possible, by giving Miranda scripts to illustrate its input and its output.

The first section below describes parsing, a transformation which adds structural information to a script by converting it from text into a syntax tree. The second section describes dependency analysis, which simplifies a script by sorting function definitions into an order suitable for subsequent processing, according to the way in which the definitions depend on each other. The third section describes type inference, a process which adds type information to a script by finding and checking the types of all the subexpressions. The fourth section describes a collection of simplifications which can be carried out to eliminate high level language features from a script. Finally, the last section describes briefly some of the optimisations which can be performed at a high level before code generation begins.

Some of the techniques described, particularly in the parsing section, are the same as those used in procedural languages compilers, and have been extensively studied – see Aho & Ullman [2], for example. However, many of the techniques are unique to functional languages, and are quite recent and not widely known. For more information about these, see the books by Peyton Jones [9] and by Field & Harrison [6].

## 6.1 Parsing

To **parse** a script means to analyse its structure and convert it from text into a syntax tree. Parsing can be thought of as a two stage process. The first stage is to split the text into symbols. The second is to convert the symbols into a tree, according to the syntax rules of the language.

### 6.1.1 Tokens and Symbols

The first stage of parsing is called **lexical analysis**, and involves splitting up the text of a script into a stream of tokens. A **token** is the smallest unit of text with an independent meaning, e.g. an identifier or operator.

To find out where each token begins and ends, the characters are classi-fied as letters, digits, punctuation marks etc. The class of the first character of a token determines what kind of token it is, and thus how far it extends. For example, if the first character is a letter, then the token is an identifier or keyword, and continues with letters, digits, underscores and quotes.

At the same time as dividing the text into tokens, the parser discards comments and adds the semicolons which are implied by the layout of the script, according to the offside rule mentioned in Section 2.7.

To find out where semicolons should be added, the parser keeps track of all incomplete definitions and declarations, and the columns in which their right hand sides begin. Whenever a new line begins to the left of a right hand side, a semicolon is added to terminate the incomplete construct. The process can be illustrated with the following script:

```
f n
=    a*n+b  where
     a  =  2
     b  =  3              || end of definition of b and of f

g x  =  x
```

If the resulting stream of tokens is printed out with all the tokens on one line, and with single spaces separating them, the result is a perfectly valid Miranda script which is equivalent to the original:

```
f n = a * n + b where a = 2 ; b = 3 ; ; g x = x ;
```

This new version of the script illustrates the processing which has been performed. The spaces indicate where each token ends and the next begins, and explicit semicolons take the place of the implicit layout rules. Before the definition of *g*, two semicolons have been inserted, one to terminate the definition of *b* and one to terminate the definition of *f*, because the definition of *g* begins to the left of the column containing *3* and the column containing *a*.

Some language constructs, such as **where** clauses, list comprehensions and patterns, allow new identifiers to be introduced. A single script can thus contain several different definitions or declarations for the same token, each with a different scope. For example, in the script:

```
x  =  10
f x  =  x
```

there are two different versions of *x*. One corresponds to the first definition, and has global scope, while the second is a parameter whose scope is just the second definition. A token associated with a particular definition or declaration is called a **symbol**, so that in the above example, there are two different symbols with the name *x*.

Each occurrence of a token in a script has to be matched up to the correct definition or declaration. This involves constructing a symbol table for each scope, and looking up each token in the relevant symbol table. This can be regarded as a transformation in which tokens are renamed to make them unique though, in practice, information is usually added to the syntax tree during syntax analysis giving the relevant definition or declaration for each token.

## 6.1.2   Syntax

The syntax rules for a language are often given as stylised equations defining each of the constructs of the language. For example, the syntax of type declarations might be represented by the rule:

$$type\_decl \quad = \quad id\_list \quad "::" \quad type\_expr \quad ";"$$

which says that a type declaration consists of a list of identifiers, followed by the symbol : :, followed by a type expression, followed by a semicolon.

The second stage of parsing is to construct a syntax tree which describes the structure of the script according to these rules. There are many different techniques used for this in procedural compilers, but the simplest and most natural one is called **recursive descent**. As well as being simple, it is also quite efficient – it takes an amount of time proportional to the number of symbols processed.

With this technique, each construct is represented by a function which takes a list of symbols as its argument. The list of symbols is assumed to begin with an example of the given construct, and the function returns a pair containing a tree structure representing the construct, and the list of remaining symbols. For example, the syntax rule shown above leads to a function *type_decl* for analysing type declarations. A simplified version of the function might be:

```
type_decl ts
=   (Tree "::" [lhs,rhs], rts)   where
    (lhs, ("::" : rts1))   =   id_list ts
    (rhs, (";" : rts))   =   type_expr rts1
```

For simplicity, it is assumed that symbols are strings, and that syntax trees are trees of the type described in Section 4.5, with strings as labels. The result tree has the symbol : : as its label, and has two subtrees representing the left and right hand sides of the declaration. The function *id_list* is used to find the left hand side and create a tree from it. The remaining symbols are assumed to begin with : : which is discarded, and then the function *type_expr* is used to create a tree representing the right hand side. Finally, the terminating semicolon is discarded so that the second item *rts* in the final result represents the list of symbols following the type declaration.

Sometimes, this simple recursive descent technique has to be extended by looking ahead or backtracking. For example, the syntax rule for definitions might state that a definition is either a function definition or a type definition:

```
defn  =  fun_defn | type_defn
```

The corresponding function *defn* can determine which kind of definition is present by looking ahead in the symbol list to see if the main symbol of the definition is = or *::=*. Alternatively, and more generally, all the syntax functions can return an additional indication of success or failure. Then *defn* can call *fun_defn* to see if it succeeds, and then backtrack by calling *type_defn* on the original symbol list only if the call to *fun_defn* fails.

These extensions to simple recursive descent mean that the method may take more than a linear amount of time. There are other, more sophisticated, methods which can deal with these problems in linear time. However, in practice, the inefficiency involved is usually negligible compared to the total time taken to compile a script, and recursive descent with backtracking is often the method chosen for functional language compilers.

When parsing expressions, operator precedences have to be taken into account. This can be done by having a separate construct for each precedence level. For example, syntax rules for simple numerical expressions might include:

```
expr   =  term | expr "+" term | expr "-" term
term   =  factor | term "*" factor | term "/" factor
factor =  simple_expr | simple_expr "^" factor
```

The first rule says that an expression is either a single term, or else a number of terms joined by + and - operators in a left associative way so that, for example, *a-b+c* means *(a-b)+c*. The second rule similarly specifies that a term consists of factors joined by * and / operators. The third rule states that factors are formed from simple expressions using the ^ operator, this time in a right associative way.

The function corresponding to each equation can be defined as a loop. For example, *expr* can repeatedly call *term* to extract terms from the list

of symbols, until it finds no more + or − operators, attaching the new term
to the current tree each time round the loop.

An alternative to having a separate function for each precedence level is
to have a single function with an extra argument representing the current
precedence level, and to use a table containing the precedence information
for each operator.

The result of syntax analysis is a tree in which the nodes represent
language constructs, identifiers, operators and so on. For example, if a script
contains a function *iter* (equivalent to the standard *iterate* function)
with the definition:

```
iter f x  =  x : iter f (f x)
```

then the definition might be represented by the following tree, in which =
is used to indicate a function definition, @ is used to indicate a function
application, and *i* is used as an abbreviation for *iter*:

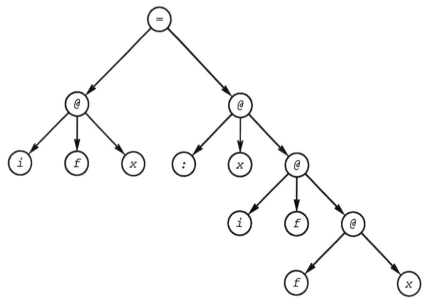

All the remaining transformations in this chapter are carried out on tree
structures of this kind. However, we will continue to describe them as source
to source transformations where appropriate.

## 6.2  Dependency

The next transformation which a compiler needs to do is **dependency analysis**. This involves re-ordering the definitions in a script so that functions

are defined before they are used. This is vital to make later processing steps, particularly type inference, work smoothly.

As an example of dependency analysis, suppose we have a script in which four identifiers *a*, *b*, *c* and *d* have definitions of the form:

```
a   =   ... c ... d ...
b   =   ... a ... d ...
c   =   ...
d   =   ... a ... c ...
```

Only the information relevant to dependency analysis is shown here. For example the first line indicates that the definition of *a* mentions *c* and *d*, and so *a* is said to **depend** on *c* and *d*.

The dependency information in these definitions can be pictured in the form of a directed graph. The graph has a node for each identifier and an edge for each pair of identifiers where the first depends on the second:

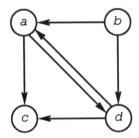

It is easy to see how the definitions should be re-ordered so that no identifier is used before its definition. The definition for *c* must come first because *c* does not depend on anything else, but everything depends directly or indirectly on *c*. Next come *a* and *d*, which depend on each other – they might be mutually recursive functions for example – and so must be processed together. Finally comes *b*. The result of dependency analysis is equivalent to transforming the script into the form:

```
c     =   ...
(a,d)  =   (... c ... d ..., ... a ... c ...)
b     =   ... a ... d ...
```

Dependency information can be obtained using the depth first search technique described in Section 4.8. The function *search* defined there takes a graph and a list of nodes, and produces a list of trees which include all the nodes reachable from the given nodes. Thus, given a dependency graph *g* of the form shown above, all the identifiers on which a given identifier *x* depends can be found using the function:

```
depend g x  =  flatten (hd (search g [x]))
```

By calling this function repeatedly, once for each identifier, complete dependency information can be obtained. However, the ordering of the identifiers
still has to be determined.

It turns out that the ordering of the identifiers can be obtained efficiently
without computing the complete dependency information. The problem is
to find the mutually recursive groups of identifiers, and then sort the groups
into order. In graph theory terminology, such mutually recursive groups
form **strong components** of the graph, i.e. components within which every
node can be reached from every other.

A single depth first search checks for reachability in only one direction.
However, if the edges of the graph are reversed with the *invert* function,
and a second search is carried out using the ordering of the nodes produced
by the first search, then the graph is broken into its strong components. A
function *components* which does this can be defined by:

```
components g
=  [flatten t | t <- search2]  where

   search1  =  search g (nodes g)
   ordering  =  concat [flatten t | t <- search1]
   search2  =  search (invert g) ordering
```

A procedural version of this algorithm, together with an explanation of
why it works, is described by Aho, Hopcroft and Ullman [3]. Remarkably,
the algorithm not only produces the required components, it also produces
them in the right order. For example, applied to the dependency graph
pictured above, it gives the result *[[c],[a,d],[b]]* which is exactly the
information required to re-order the definitions in the original script.

The procedural version of the algorithm takes an amount of time linear
in the number edges of the graph. The functional version presented here can
also be made to run in linear time, provided that the set functions *insert*
and *element*, and the graph function *neighbours*, can be made to run
in constant time. As discussed in Chapter 4, this is possible in a language
which has structures for constant time lookup and update.

## 6.3   Type Inference

The purpose of types is to catch errors at compile time rather than run time,
where possible, and to provide the compiler with information which it can

use for optimisation. In a typical procedural language, every identifier has to have its type declared when it is defined, and then the compiler checks that every use of that identifier is consistent with its type. This is called **type checking**. In functional languages, types need not be declared at all. The compiler infers the types of identifiers from their definitions, as well as checking their uses. This is called **type inference**.

Type inference can be regarded as a transformation in which type declarations are added to a script. For example, suppose a script contains a definition of a function *iter*, as mentioned in Section 6.1.2:

```
iter f x  =  x : iter f (f x)
```

Then the action of the type inference algorithm is equivalent to adding a type declaration for it to the script:

```
iter  ::  (*->*)->*->[*]
```

This declaration indicates that for any given type *T*, the function *iter* takes a function of type *T->T*, together with a value of type *T*, and produces as result a list of items of type *T*.

These type declarations can be regarded as **annotations**, i.e. as declarations added to a script which do not change its meaning, but which provide information about it for the benefit of the compiler. The programmer can include type declarations in a script – the compiler then checks that they are consistent with the types which it infers for itself. Annotations of other kinds, both automatically generated and programmer defined, are quite often used in functional language compilers.

The type inference algorithm is often called the Hindley-Milner algorithm after its inventors. Before describing the algorithm, we will first look at polymorphism and the way in which it interacts with dependency analysis.

## 6.3.1  Polymorphism

Types can be regarded as sets of values. The type inference algorithm relies on the fact that, for the most part, these sets are disjoint, so that a value typically has a unique type. With polymorphism, a value may not always have a unique type, but it still has a unique most general type.

For example, the list *[42]* has the unique type *[num]*, but the empty list *[]* belongs to all list types such as *[bool]*, *[num]*, *[[num]]*, *[num->bool]*, and so on. However, *[]* belongs to a unique most general type *[*]* meaning "list of any type". A value belonging to a polymorphic type must have very general properties, and so a polymorphic type contains a very restricted set of values. For example, a value belonging to *[*]* must be compatible with lists of every kind, i.e. it must belong to every concrete list type. In fact *[]* is essentially the only value of type *[*]* (except for partial values involving ⊥, see Chapter 8).

As another example, the *reverse* function has the type *[*]->[*]*. Again, a function of this type must be very general. It must be capable of processing any kind of list, returning a list of the same kind. The only functions of this type are ones such as *reverse*, *tl* or *init* which re-arrange the items in a list without "looking inside" them.

A polymorphic function can be used on arguments of different types in the same script. For example, *reverse* can be used on a list of characters, and on a list of numbers, in close proximity:

```
result  =  (reverse "abc", reverse [1..3])
```

Now, we will look at some examples which illustrate the limitations of the type inference system, and which also illustrate the relevance of dependency analysis. First, a function cannot be used on different types within its own definition. It can only be used on values of the same type as its argument, though this may be an unknown type. For example, a definition such as the following is illegal:

```
f x  =  ... f "abc" ... f [1..3] ...
```

Second, a function cannot be used on different types within the group of mutually recursive functions which contains it. For example, the following is illegal:

```
f x  =  ... g x ...
g x  =  ... f "abc" ... f [1..3] ...
```

Finally, a function which is passed as an argument cannot be used on different types. For example, the following is illegal:

```
g f  =  ... f "abc" ... f [1..3] ...
```

These restrictions on polymorphism are necessary in order for the type inference algorithm described here to work. Even with the restrictions, the type system is powerful, flexible and unobtrusive.

Type inference is done on the definitions in the order determined by dependency analysis, with a mutually recursive group of definitions being processed together. This ensures that a polymorphic function can be used on different types in any context other than those mentioned above.

## 6.3.2   The Type Inference Algorithm

When the processing of a function definition begins, the subexpressions appearing in the definition are allocated types. This can be done by attaching a type to each node in the syntax tree. Most of these types are initially unknown, so type variables $T1$, $T2$, ... are introduced for these unknown types. For example, take the definition of the function *iter* mentioned earlier:

```
iter f x  =  x : iter f (f x)
```

An initial type is attached to each node of the subtrees representing the left and right hand sides of the equation. As before, $i$ is used as an abbreviation for *iter*:

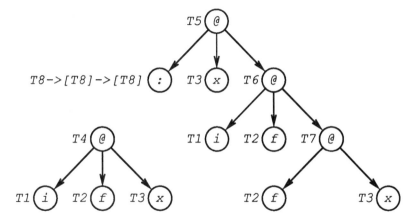

The nodes represent subexpressions which fall into three categories. First, there are identifiers whose types are to be determined, in this case the function name *iter* and the parameters $f$ and $x$, which are allocated type variables $T1$ to $T3$. Each of these identifiers is given the same type every time it occurs. Second, there are compound subexpressions, such as the left hand side *iter f x*. These are allocated type variables $T4$ to $T7$. Finally, there are global identifiers. Their types are known, because dependency analysis ensures that their definitions have already been processed. If their types are polymorphic, then they are given different types, using fresh type variables, each time they occur. In the example, the only global identifier is `:` with type `*->[*]->[*]`. Its one occurrence is allocated the type `T8->[T8]->[T8]`. If there had been a second occurrence, it would be given the type `T9->[T9]->[T9]`, and so on.

During the inference algorithm, type expressions are represented as trees containing variables, and information is gathered about the variables by matching up pairs of type expressions using the unification algorithm, as described in Section 5.5.2. The pair *(T4, T5)* is matched because the left and right hand sides of the equation must have the same type. Also, a pair is matched for each function application. For example, in the left hand side expression *iter f x*, the type *T1* of *iter* must be a function taking two arguments of types *T2* and *T3*, and returning a result of type *T4*. Thus five pairs of types are matched in all:

```
(T4,  T5)
(T1,  T2->T3->T4)
(T8->[T8]->[T8],  T3->T6->T5)
(T1,  T2->T7->T6)
(T2,  T3->T7)
```

The total information obtained from matching these pairs is:

```
T1   =   (T3->T3)->T3->[T3]        T5   =   [T3]
T2   =   T3->T3                     T6   =   [T3]
T3   =   T3                         T7   =   T3
T4   =   [T3]                       T8   =   T3
```

No information has been obtained about the type variable *T3*, but all the other type variables have been determined as expressions using *T3*. The fact that *T3* has not been determined means that the definition of *iter* is correct whatever *T3* is replaced by. Thus, *T3* can be turned into a polymorphic parameter, and the type of *iter* can be deduced as *(\*->\*)->\*->[\*]* from the information gained about *T1*, and *iter* can be used in a polymorphic way in subsequent definitions.

## 6.4  Simplification

The transformations described in this section are simplifications, each of which involves translating some high level feature of the language into lower level features. Thus a script gets translated into an equivalent one which uses only a small subset of the language, for which it is easier to generate code.

The higher level features of Miranda which we will consider simplifying are list expressions, guards, local definitions and pattern matching.

## 6.4.1 List Expressions

The commonest kind of compound expression in Miranda is a function application. One aim of simplification is to reduce other language features to applications of suitable built-in functions. List expressions, including ranges and list comprehensions, provide examples of expressions which can be transformed into such function applications.

An explicit list such as *[a,b,c]* is simply translated into the form *a:b:c:[]*, which is equivalent to *a:(b:(c:[]))* and so consists of several applications of the *:* constructor.

A range of the form *[m..n]*, which is an abbreviation for the list of numbers from *m* up to *n* inclusive, can be translated into a function application *range m n* where *range* is a function defined by:

> *range m n*
> *=   [],                        if m > n*
> *=   m : range (m+1) n,    otherwise*

Of course, when introducing a new function such as *range* into a script as part of a source to source transformation, it must be given a name which does not clash with any other identifier in the script. Other range notations such as *[m0,m1..n]* with an explicit stepsize, or *[m..]* representing an infinite range, can be dealt with by introducing similar functions.

The list comprehension notation was described in Section 2.3.1. A list comprehension is an expression such as *[m+n | m<-ms; m>0; n<-ns]* consisting of a result expression and a sequence of qualifiers, each qualifier being a generator or a filter. As described in Chapter 3, using the list comprehension notation is equivalent to using the standard functions *map*, *filter* and *concat*, and indeed it is possible to translate a list comprehension into applications of these functions. For example, a list comprehension such as the one above in which the first qualifier is a generator and the second is a filter can be translated into:

> *concat (map f (filter g ms))*  **where**
> *f m   =   [m+n | n<-ns]*
> *g m   =   m>0*

This transformation has eliminated the first generator, and can be applied recursively to the remaining list comprehension *[m+n | n<-ns]* to complete the transformation. The functions *f* and *g* are newly introduced ones which must be given names distinct from any identifiers with which they might clash.

A transformation such as this one involves replacing a simple expression by another expression with a **where** clause attached. Miranda does not allow **where** clauses to be attached to arbitrary subexpressions, but only to complete right hand sides. Thus, for the result to be a valid Miranda program, the new definitions which are introduced have to be put into a **where** clause attached to the right hand side within which the subexpression being translated is embedded.

This transformation for list comprehensions is not the most efficient one possible. As with the tree operations discussed in Section 4.5, multiple uses of the `concat` function for separate generators can lead to a situation in which it takes more than a constant time to generate each item. To avoid this, list comprehensions can be transformed directly into functions. For example, the list comprehension `[(x,y) | x<-xs; y<-ys]` can be translated into:

```
f xs   where
f []   =   []
f (x:rxs)
=   g ys   where
    g []   =   f rxs
    g (y:rys)   =   (x,y) : g rys
```

The functions `f` and `g`, and the local parameters `rxs` and `rys` are newly introduced names which must not clash with any which already exist. The function `f` runs through the list `xs`, calling `g` for each member. The function `g` runs through the list `ys` generating result items. When `g` finishes, it returns to the evaluation of `f`. The function `g` appears in a separate local **where** clause because its definition depends on `x` and `rxs`.

If an optimal translation of this form is used, then it becomes appropriate to define the `map`, `filter` and `concat` functions in terms of list comprehensions, instead of the other way round. Indeed, that is how they are defined in Appendix B.

### 6.4.2   Guards

To transform a definition which includes guards, we just need a `test` function. For example, the factorial function defined by:

```
fac n
=   1,                if n=0
=   n * fac(n-1),   otherwise
```

is simply replaced by:

```
fac n  =  test (n=0) 1 (n * fac (n-1))
```

The *test* function is just an *if...then...else...*function with three arguments. It returns either its second or third argument according to whether its first argument is *True* or *False*. It can be defined by pattern matching as:

```
test True x y  =  x
test False x y  =  y
```

One of the reasons that Miranda has a special notation for guards, rather than using a function like *test*, is that conditionals are allowed to interact with pattern matching. For example, it would be possible to define the standard function *drop* by:

```
drop n xs
=  error "fractional",  if ~ integer n
=  xs,                  if n<=0 \/ xs=[]
drop (n+1) (x:rxs)  =  drop n rxs
```

If neither of the guards in the first equation succeed, then the second equation is used. The subtleties of translating guards when they interact with pattern matching in this way will not be described here.

### 6.4.3 Local Definitions

One possible transformation for eliminating local definitions is called **lifting**. This means taking definitions from inside a **where** clause and lifting them out so that they become global definitions at the outermost level. The main subtlety in doing this is that the local definitions may depend on the arguments to the main function. For example, the standard *sqrt* function can be defined (roughly) by:

```
sqrt x
=  until near improve (x/2)  where
     near r  =  abs (r^2 - x) < 1e-12
     improve r  =  (r + x/r)/2
```

Here both local functions *near* and *improve* depend on the parameter *x*. When compiling code for these local functions, it is not immediately clear how they are going to be able to access *x*. The problem is even more acute for nested **where** clauses in which an innermost function may depend on the argument parameters of functions at several outer levels.

There are known run-time solutions to this problem, but the lifting transformation provides a convenient compile-time solution. The idea is to add extra arguments to the local functions so that they are passed all the variables they need for execution.

In the *sqrt* example, *x* is added as an extra (first) argument to *near* and *improve* everywhere they appear. These two functions become self-contained, and can be lifted to the top level, renaming them to avoid name clashes if necessary.

```
sqrt x  =  until (near' x) (improve' x) (x/2)
near' x r  =  abs (r^2 - x) < 1e-12
improve' x r  =  (r + x/r)/2
```

The expressions *near'* x and *improve'* x are partially applied functions waiting for a second argument, as described in Section 2.4.4.

There are many subtleties in optimising this process in practice. For example, the number of extra arguments needs to be kept to a minimum. The variables which need to be added as extra arguments are those on which the local function depends, directly or indirectly. Such information can be obtained from a dependency analysis algorithm, as described in Section 6.2. For example, a function *addsq* which adds the square of a given number to each member of a given list can be defined by:

```
addsq m []  =  []
addsq m (n:rns)
  =  f n : addsq m rns   where
       f p  =  sq + p
       sq  =  m^2
```

All three parameters *m*, *n* and *rns* are potential extra arguments to *f* and *sq*. However, *sq* depends only on *m*. Since *sq* will have to have *m* added as an extra argument, and since *f* mentions *sq*, the function *f* too depends (indirectly) on *m*. Adding *m* as an extra argument to *f* and *sq* and lifting gives:

```
addsq m []  =  []
```

```
addsq m (n:rns)  =  f' m n : addsq m rns
f' m p  =  sq' m + p
sq' m  =  m^2
```

There are many more details to be taken into account in optimising the lifting process. For example, the ordering of the added arguments can be important in interactions with other optimisations, and there are techniques which help to maximise the amount of sharing which can be achieved. Sharing will be discussed in more detail in Section 6.5.2.

### 6.4.4  Patterns

It is possible to eliminate pattern matching by using functions to test and break down data values. As described in Section 2.3.3, every type can be thought of as consisting of a number of different kinds of structure, each kind built with a particular constructor. Each type can be provided with a built-in *switch* function which distinguishes between the constructors, and a number of built-in field extraction functions.

For example, pattern matching on lists can be eliminated using a new built-in function *switchlist*, which returns its second or third argument according to whether its first argument is empty or non-empty, and the standard functions *hd* and *tl*, which are now regarded as built-in. A simple definition such as:

```
squares []  =  []
squares (n:rns)  =  n^2 : squares rns
```

can be transformed into:

```
squares ns
=  switchlist ns [] ((hd ns)^2 : squares (tl ns))
```

In practice, many compilers do not do this transformation, because suitable code can be generated directly from the original definition. A simple pattern match, i.e. one which involves checking a value to see which constructor it is built from, without processing the fields, corresponds to a single evaluation step. Whether the transformation to function applications is carried out or not, more complicated cases of pattern matching need to be simplified into multiple uses of simple pattern matching, and this needs to be done in a way which is as efficient as possible. For example, several arguments may be described by patterns, as in the definition:

```
f [] ys  =  0
f (x:rxs) []  =  1
f (x:rxs) (y:rys)  =  2
```

This is translated into two simpler pattern matches, one on the first argument *xs*, and then one on the second argument *ys* if the first argument is non-empty:

```
f xs ys  =  switchlist xs 0 (switchlist ys 1 2)
```

A similar situation arises when the patterns themselves are complicated. For example, a function *g* might be defined by:

```
g []  =  0
g [x]  =  1
g (x:y:rys)  =  2
```

This can be transformed into two simple pattern matches, the first to check the argument *xs*, and second to check the tail *rxs* if *xs* is non-empty:

```
g xs
=  switchlist xs 0 (switchlist (tl xs) 1 2)
```

There are further complications to do with default cases, the ordering of equations, constants appearing in the patterns, parameters appearing repeatedly, the interaction with guards and so on. See Peyton Jones [9] for a fuller story.

## 6.5   Optimisations

There are many optimisations which can be performed at a high level on functional programs, either by transforming them, or else by analysing them to extract extra information which can be added as annotations and passed on to the code generation phase.

The algorithms which are used for carrying out optimisations tend to be rather subtle, and we will not describe them in detail here. One powerful technique which can be used for analysing programs in a wide variety of different situations is **abstract interpretation**. Roughly speaking, this involves executing the program symbolically, not using actual values, but using instead abstract symbols which represent properties of those values. For details, see Abramsky & Hankin [1].

The optimisations described here are strictness, sharing, and re-use.

## 6.5.1   Strictness

Strictness is the opposite of laziness. As pointed out in Section 1.3.2, laziness is an essential property of pure functional languages, and it permeates this book. Function arguments are passed as unevaluated expressions, and their evaluation is delayed until their value is required. However, there is an implementation cost in doing this – in order to delay the evaluation of an expression, code has to be generated to create and manipulate structures which represent unevaluated expressions, as described in the next chapter.

If it is known that a particular function argument will definitely be evaluated once the function is called, it does no harm to evaluate the argument before the call. This may eliminate the need to generate code to represent and manipulate the argument as an unevaluated expression. The gathering of this kind of information about functions is called **strictness analysis**. The information can be passed in the form of annotations to the code generator, which can use it to improve the quality of the code generated. For example, the function *test* introduced in Section 6.4.1 is defined by:

```
test  True  x y  =  x
test  False x y  =  y
```

It is easy to see from this definition that the first argument of *test* is evaluated, but not necessarily the second or third. Pattern matching is used on the first argument, so it must be evaluated in order to determine which equation to use. Neither the second nor the third argument necessarily appears in the result, so neither of them is necessarily evaluated.

Strictness analysis can also determine to what extent expressions need to be evaluated. The smallest amount of evaluation which can be done on an expression is **head-evaluation**. This means evaluating an expression just far enough to determine the main constructor, but not necessarily its fields. For example, if a single evaluation step is performed on the unevaluated expression *[1..10]*, the result is the head-evaluated expression *1:[2..10]*. This is enough to determine that the main constructor is *:* but its second field *[2..10]* is still an unevaluated expression. More details about evaluation will be given in the next chapter.

A function is said to be **strict** in one of its arguments if that argument will definitely be head-evaluated or, to be more precise, if head-evaluation of that argument before a call makes no difference to the behaviour of the function. For example, the standard function *map* is defined by:

```
map f xs  =  [f x | x<-xs]
```

This is strict in the second argument, although the second argument is not necessarily fully evaluated, depending on what is done with the result of the call. The fact that head-evaluating the second argument makes no difference to the behaviour of the function means that the following definition for *map* is equivalent to the one above:

```
map f xs  =  seq xs [f x | x<-xs]
```

The standard *seq* function makes sure that the evaluation of its first argument begins before evaluation of its second. To do this, it performs a single evaluation step on its first argument, i.e. head-evaluates it, and then returns its second argument. The *seq* function may be used in this way as an annotation which does not change the behaviour of the *map* function, but which signals the strictness property of the function to the code generator.

Strictness can be difficult to determine. For example, a loop function *count* described in Section 3.2.1 has the definition:

```
count n []  =  n
count n (x:rxs)  =  count (n+1) rxs
```

This function is strict in $n$, but the fact depends on knowing that the recursion terminates (on finite lists), and that evaluation of the result expression then forces evaluation of the original argument $n$. In the case of an infinite list as the second argument, the recursion would fail to terminate – it would get stuck in an infinite loop. The only way in which evaluation of the first argument before the call could affect the result would be if it represented an error value, in which case that error would occur instead of the infinite loop. It is usual to treat all errors, including infinite loops, as equal (see Chapter 8), so the function can be regarded as strict in $n$.

Strictness analysis may be unable to detect cases of strictness such as this one, and indeed there is no algorithm for finding all possible cases of strictness. Any function argument which is not definitely determined to be strict during analysis has to be treated as an unevaluated expression. For this reason, some languages allow the programmer to add strictness annotations which can be used for optimisation purposes. For example, the second equation in the definition of *count* could be changed by the programmer to read:

```
count n (x:rxs)  =  seq n (count (n+1) rxs)
```

to signal to the compiler that the *count* function is indeed strict in $n$.

There are cases in which efficiency can be improved by making a non-strict function into a strict one. For example, a function *foldl'* very similar to the standard *foldl* function can be defined by:

```
foldl' op c []     =  c
foldl' op c (x:rxs)  =  foldl' op (c $op x) rxs
```

With this definition, *foldl'* is not strict in its second argument *c*, as can be seen by evaluating the following expression. The standard error value *undef* is passed as the second argument. If this were evaluated, a program error would be reported, whereas in fact the evaluation terminates successfully:

```
?  foldl' (converse (\/)) undef [True]
True
```

The standard function *converse* takes a function of two arguments and returns a similar function which accepts its arguments in reverse order. Since the standard boolean operator \/ is not strict in its second argument, *converse* (\/) is a version of \/ which is not strict in its first argument, and so the above expression returns a result without evaluating *undef*.

However, *foldl'* only fails to evaluate its second argument in very unusual circumstances, such as the above, and the function uses up memory space unnecessarily in storing a larger and larger unevaluated expression in the second argument. For this reason, the standard function *foldl* is defined to be strict in *c*, even though this changes the behaviour slightly. This can be signalled by adding a strictness annotation to its definition:

```
foldl op c []   =   c
foldl op c (x:rxs)
= seq c (foldl op (c $op x) rxs)
```

Current versions of the Miranda compiler do not recognise this use of *seq* as a strictness annotation, and indeed its use may spoil other optimisations and lead to a less efficient implementation, so in practice *foldl* is given a built-in implementation equivalent to the one shown here.

## 6.5.2 Sharing

One of the key features of a good implementation of a functional language is the sharing of subexpressions so that they are only evaluated once. In Section 2.6.1, this sharing was accomplished by a version of reduction in

which local definitions were used to represent shared subexpressions.  A
programmer can indicate sharing in a similar way in a program by using
local definitions. For example, in the definition:

```
split xs
    =   (take (#xs div 2) xs, drop (#xs div 2) xs)
```

the subexpression #xs *div* 2 is mentioned twice and would probably be
evaluated twice. On the other hand, if the definition is re-written as:

```
split xs
    =   (take half xs, drop half xs)   where
         half  =   #xs div 2
```

then the subexpression is mentioned only once, and the compiler will only
generate code to evaluate it once.

It is important when lifting, as described in Section 6.4.3, not to lift
the definitions of constants such as *half*, otherwise they become functions
which are called repeatedly, which spoils the sharing effect. Such constant
definitions can be left in place and dealt with directly by the code generator.

There are situations in which the compiler itself needs to make transformations like the one above in order to ensure that expressions are only
evaluated once. For example, suppose a script contains the definition:

```
echo  =   interleave $- $-
```

where *interleave* is some function which interleaves two streams by taking alternate members from each. It is vital that $- is only evaluated once,
so that the two occurrences of $- represent the same input stream which is
read in only once. This can be done by transforming the definition to:

```
echo  =   interleave input input   where   input = $-
```

Another situation where sharing is often desirable is where a function
definition contains a constant expression. For example, the function *addsq*
defined in Section 6.4.3 which adds the square of a number to each member
of a list could be defined by:

```
addsq m ns
    =   [f n | n<-ns]   where
         f n  =   m^2 + n
```

In one call to *addsq*, the local function *f* may be called many times, and on each call it may re-compute $m\hat{}2$. However, the expression $m\hat{}2$ is the same on each call to *f*, and so can be computed separately by transforming the definition of *addsq* to:

```
addsq m ns
 =   [f n | n<-ns]   where
     f n  =  sq + n
     sq   =  m^2
```

To lift the definition of *f*, but not the constant *sq*, *sq* is added as an extra argument to *f*:

```
addsq m ns
 =   [f' sq n | n<-ns]   where   sq  =  m^2
     f' sq n  =  sq + n
```

This extraction of constant subexpressions is usually combined with the lifting process, since they are so intimately connected. In the above example, the overall effect is to add the constant subexpression $m\hat{}2$ rather than the parameter *m* as an extra argument to *f*.

A further complication is that there may be constant subexpressions inside the definitions of functions which are created dynamically, i.e. while a program is running. One example arises in creating **memo** functions, i.e. functions which remember results which they have produced in the past, so as to avoid recomputing them. Suppose that it is found that a function *f* is particularly expensive to compute, so that it is worth remembering previous results. What is wanted is the ability to use instead an equivalent function which first checks its argument against some stored answers for which it can return the result immediately, and which calls the original function *f* only if this fails. To support such memo functions, we can provide a general purpose function *memo* defined by:

```
memo f x
 =   g   where
     g y  =  test (y=x) (f x) (f y)
```

The first argument *f* is a function which is to be updated so that it remembers its result for argument *x*. The *memo* function returns a new version *g* of *f* which tests its argument *y* against *x* and immediately returns the constant expression *f x* if the test succeeds. Otherwise it calls the original function *f* on its argument.

The success of this idea depends on the fact that the constant expression
*f x* inside the definition of *g* need only be computed once after *g* is created.
To ensure this, it can be added as an extra argument to *g* as *g* is lifted to
form *g′*. The result returned from *memo* is then a partial application of the
function *g′*:

```
memo f x  =  g' (f x) f x
g' z f x y  =   test (y=x) z (f y)
```

The code generator must ensure that whenever such a partial application
is created, the argument expressions passed in are properly shared so that
they are never evaluated more than once.

In practice, *memo* would be called repeatedly to create a function which
remembers many different result values. There are programs for which memo
functions can provide considerable improvements in efficiency (the technique
is sometimes called "dynamic programming"). As described here, the programmer has to choose which result values to remember. Some compilers
arrange for ordinary functions to be converted into memo functions which
remember all the results which they produce, as far as the available memory
allows, whenever requested by some programmer annotation.

If constant expressions are added as extra arguments during lifting in
this way, and a suitable code generator is used, the implementation of the
language can be made **fully lazy**. This means that the implementation is
not only lazy, but also ensures that once an expression is created, it is never
evaluated more than once. Unlike ordinary laziness, this full laziness only
affects efficiency, not the results produced.

### 6.5.3   Reuse

The analysis of **reuse** is, in a sense, the opposite of sharing. As we shall see
in the next chapter, a subexpression is shared by having several references to
it, so that any evaluation steps performed on the subexpression are shared by
those references. If it can be determined that a subexpression is not shared,
i.e. that there is only one reference to it, then when the subexpression is
no longer needed, the space occupied by it can be reused for some other
purpose. For example, the definition of the loop function *count* discussed
earlier in the chapter is:

```
count n []  =  n
count n (x:rxs)  =  count (n+1) rxs
```

Suppose that, when this function is first called, a copy is made of the argument *n* so that there is only one reference to it. When the function is called recursively, the argument *n* is used to form the new value *n+1*, and there are no further references to the old *n*. Thus the space occupied by *n* can be reused to hold the value *n+1*.

This kind of local analysis of reuse within a single function definition is usually done as part of code generation. However, more general methods of analysing reuse allow data structures to be updated in place and thus retain their identity globally beyond just a single function definition. These considerations lead to several possible methods for the efficient implementation of tables and arrays.

Even without analysis of reuse, it is possible to implement tables and arrays without copying. Suppose a call *update t k v'* updates a structure *t* by associating a new value *v'* with the key or index *k*. This can be implemented by remembering the old value *v* associated with key *k* before the call and updating *t* in place to form *t'*. The old structure *t* can be replaced with an expression of the form *update t' k v* which, if evaluated, would make the structure revert to its former value.

If a structure is used in a **single threaded** way, that is in such a way that there are never any references to old versions of the structure, then the unevaluated expressions in the above implementation are never evaluated, and operations take a constant amount of time. If the structure is not used in a single threaded way, the implementation provides less efficient, but still correct, operations.

The operations in this implementation take several times longer than corresponding procedural ones. Analysis of reuse can be used to determine situations in which structures are used in a single threaded way, and can thus remove the need to create the unevaluated expressions. This makes the operations as efficient as procedural ones.

The problem with relying on analysis of reuse for efficiency in this way is that it is not possible for a compiler to detect all possible cases of single threading. Thus there is also a need for language constructs which enforce single threaded use of structures.

One way of doing this is to have read-only structures which cannot be updated at all. The entries in such structures are allowed to be expressions which are evaluated lazily, and which can depend on each other. This makes read-only structures much more powerful than they appear at first sight, but they are still not suitable for all applications. Another way to ensure single threading, suggested by some promising recent research, is to provide an abstract data type which allows only very tightly controlled, single threaded access to the structures. Such an abstract type can then be safely implemented using update in place.

## 6.6   Exercises

1. Draw the syntax tree which results from parsing the equation:

   ```
   rep n x  =  take n (repeat x)
   ```

   Show how the type inference algorithm is used to deduce the type of *rep*.

2. Complete the transformation of the expression *[m+n | m<-ms; m>0; n<-ns]* described in Section 6.4.1 into a form which uses the functions *map*, *filter* and *concat* instead of list comprehensions.

3. Define a function *slow* which slows down the evaluation of its argument. A call *slow x* should execute a loop a number of times before returning *x*. Adjust the number of times the loop is executed so that *slow* takes an appreciable amount of time, say a couple of seconds, on your computer. Using *slow*, define a function *slowsqrt* which computes square roots inefficiently. Using the function *memo* described in Section 6.5.2, define a function *slowsqrt'* which is equivalent to *slowsqrt* except that it remembers the square root of *2*. Test this function by evaluating a list which contains several occurrences of *slowsqrt' 2* and checking that every member of the list takes a couple of seconds to appear, except for the second and subsequent occurrences of *slowsqrt' 2*.

# Chapter 7

# Low Level Implementation

In this chapter, the issues of code generation and run time support which arise in compiling functional languages are described.

The code generation process involves turning a syntax tree produced by the transformations of the previous chapter into a linear sequence of instructions. This typically involves scanning the tree to attach to each node information about the subexpression it represents such as what variables it uses, whether it is to be evaluated immediately or delayed and so on. This is followed by the generation of some code for each node to evaluate its subexpression. The techniques used are very similar to those in conventional procedural compilers, as described in Aho & Ullman[2], and can be carried out using functions akin to the *attach* and *flatten* functions described in Section 4.5.

On the other hand, the way in which values and expressions are represented, the flow of control during evaluation, and the management of memory space in functional languages are less conventional and less widely known. Thus, the emphasis of the chapter is on these issues rather than on code generation algorithms, in order to present a picture of the way in which the run time system works.

The chapter begins with a description of graph reduction, a version of reduction which forms the basis of most functional language compilers. The remainder of the chapter gives a detailed description of one particular approach to compilation, the **G-machine** approach, which uses the graph reduction idea to form a practical and efficient evaluation technique. This allows us to discuss the issues of code generation and run time support in as concrete and realistic a setting as possible.

The basic G-machine technique is quite simple and uniform and yet a variety of optimisations, some of which are mentioned in this chapter, can be incorporated to produce compilers whose efficiency approaches that of procedural language implementations. The G-machine technique can also be adapted for use on parallel computers, though only sequential computers will be considered here.

The G-machine approach to implementation is described in the books by Field & Harrison [6] and Peyton Jones [9]. The particular variation on the G-machine approach which is described in this chapter is called the **spineless, tagless G-Machine**, for reasons which will emerge in Section 7.2, and is described in a paper by Peyton Jones and Salkild [10].

At the time of writing, the current version of Miranda (release 2) uses a semi-interpretive implementation method rather than a full compiler, but a full compiler is planned for the next version and Miranda is used for the examples of source code given in the chapter. Examples of compiled code will be given in a simple, stylised assembly language. The instructions of this language will be described as they appear.

## 7.1   Graph Reduction

The reduction technique was described in Section 2.6.1 in terms of hand evaluation. The evaluation technique which is used in compiled programs, called **graph reduction**, can be regarded as an optimised version of reduction in which expressions are represented using graph-like data structures.

With reduction generally, each evaluation step consists of choosing a subexpression and replacing it by an equivalent one. For example, the first two steps of the evaluation of the expression *double (square (2+2) + 5)*, using local definitions to handle shared subexpressions, are:

```
 ?   double (square (2+2) + 5)
 →  m + m   where   m = (square (2+2) + 5)
 →  m + m   where   m = n*n + 5;   n = 2+2
```

With graph reduction, each subexpression is represented as a node, and the nodes are linked to each other with pointers. An evaluation step consists of choosing a node and overwriting it with an equivalent one. Graph reduction can be illustrated in a simplified way using a semi-textual representation of the contents of each node. For the above example, the evolution of the collection of nodes can be pictured as:

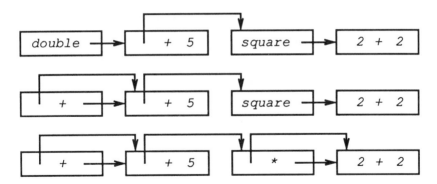

The sharing of subexpressions comes about simply by creating multiple references to the same node. When such a shared node is overwritten, all the references to it share the update. These multiple references mean that the node interconnections form a general directed graph rather than just a tree, as would be the case without sharing.

Multiple references to nodes may be created directly from the program, as well as arising from the evaluation process. Moreover, the interconnections may form cycles in some cases. For example, suppose the standard *repeat* function is defined by:

$$repeat\ x\ =\ xs\ \textbf{where}\ xs\ =\ x:xs$$

This leads to an extreme case of sharing in which an infinite list is represented as a single shared node, rather than as a chain of identical nodes which unfold as the list is evaluated. When *repeat* is called, it creates a cyclic structure to represent *xs*:

To turn the simple picture of graph reduction described so far into an efficient evaluation mechanism, particular conventions have to be chosen for representing and evaluating nodes. One particular approach to this, the G-machine approach, is described in the following sections.

The nodes are stored in a **heap** – an area of memory for storing objects with arbitrary lifetimes. The representation of the nodes is described in Section 7.2. When the heap becomes full, a garbage collection takes place to reclaim the space taken up by nodes which are no longer in use. The management of the heap is described in more detail in Section 7.4.

For efficiency, a **stack** is used to store objects with nested lifetimes. Items are removed from it explicitly when no longer needed. The stack is used to store function arguments, temporary values which are saved during calls, and return addresses. The effect is to reduce the need to store expressions explicitly in the heap, to reduce the number of times nodes get overwritten, and to organise the flow of control during evaluation.

With unoptimised graph reduction, an evaluation step consists of searching for the right node to update, and overwriting it. A node may be overwritten several times, until finally it is in an evaluated form. This corresponds to head-evaluation of the expression which the node represents – see Section 6.5.1.

The optimised evaluation mechanism described in this chapter avoids having to search for the right node to overwrite at every evaluation step. Instead, the flow of control is handled as a mixture of jumps and calls which ensure the correct order of evaluation. In addition, a node representing an unevaluated expression is only overwritten once with its final evaluated form. The way in which this is achieved is explained in Section 7.3.

## 7.2   Representation

In this section, the representations of data values, functions and unevaluated expressions used in the G-machine are described in some detail. Every node has a block of code associated with it for calculating the value which the node represents, and these blocks of code will also be described using a simple, stylised assembly language. The details of the way in which the code fragments fit together into a complete evaluation mechanism will become clear in Section 7.3.

### 7.2.1   Data Values

As described in Section 2.3.3, all data types, whether built-in or programmer defined, can be regarded as being built up out of constants and constructors. For example, lists are built from *[]* and the *:* constructor. For the purposes of this chapter, we will give these their more traditional names *Nil* and *Cons*, so the list type is defined by:

        list *   ::=   Nil | Cons * (list *)

The constants and constructors within each type can be numbered *0, 1, 2, ...* in the order in which they appear in the type definition, so that they

can be specified by a small integer **tag**. In the case of lists, *Nil* has a tag
value of *0* and a non-empty list such as *Cons x rxs* has a tag value of *1*.
Since type checking is carried out by the front end of the compiler, a data
value is completely determined at run time by its tag and its fields, if any.

One of the important representation choices is between fixed and variable
length nodes. Fixed length nodes simplify memory management, but then an
expression representing the application of a function to several arguments
must be represented by a chain of several nodes called a **spine**. In the
representation described in this chapter, a node is a variable length structure,
so that an application can be represented using a single node. Thus the
representation is called **spineless**.

A node consists of any number of **words**, each word containing a number,
an entry point in the code, or a pointer to another node. The most common
operation on a node is to **enter** it, i.e. to evaluate it and then overwrite
it with its evaluated form, if necessary. Evaluating a node corresponds to
head-evaluating the expression which it represents. To make this operation
efficient, the first word of a node, called the **label**, points to a suitable block
of code for evaluating and, if necessary, overwriting the node. In the case
of a data value, the remaining words of the node represent the fields of the
structure. The tag is not stored directly in the node, but instead is returned
by the code which the label points to. Thus the representation is called
**tagless**.

Any further information which needs to be recorded about a node, e.g.
its size and layout for memory management purposes, can be stored in the
code just before the entry point, so that it is available using a small negative
offset from the label. Nodes representing *Nil* and *Cons x rxs* look like
this:

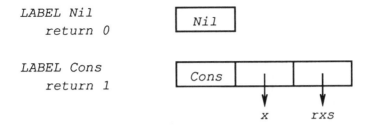

The second and third words of the *Cons* node point to other nodes in the
heap representing *x* and *rxs*. The code associated with each node consists
of a single *return* instruction which returns the tag value.

The evaluation mechanism uses two special registers, a *node* register
and a *tag* register. A node is entered by loading the *node* register with a

pointer to the node and jumping to the code label stored in the first word. If the node represents a data value, then the evaluation returns with the *node* register pointing to a suitable evaluated form of the original node, and the *tag* register holding the associated tag. The *return* instruction loads the *tag* register with the appropriate tag value and then pops a return address from the stack and jumps to it. In cases where the node is already in evaluated form, as above, the *node* register is left pointing to the same node.

For constants belonging to large enumerated types such as the *char* type, it becomes inconvenient to have a separate label for every constant. Instead, such constants can be represented by nodes with two words. The label indicates the type, and the second word contains an integer which specifies the constant. For simplicity, we will assume that the *num* type consists only of restricted integers – ones which fit in a single word – so that the *num* type can also be regarded as an enumerated type. The character *'c'* and the number *42* can be represented as:

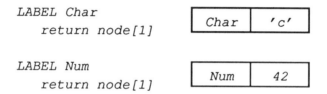

```
LABEL Char
       return node[1]

LABEL Num
       return node[1]
```

The *tag* register can be used to return a copy of the integer constant, allowing the caller to ignore the *node* register. This may fit in with optimisations in which the creation of nodes such as those shown here can sometimes be avoided.

The standard representation for data values described so far can be very inefficient on memory space. For example, if strings are represented using *Nil* and *Cons* nodes, they require five words for each character stored, three for a *Cons* node and two for a *Char* node.

In such cases, more compact non-standard representations can be used. To preserve uniformity, these compact forms can be implemented in such a way that they expand into standard representations when evaluated. This allows existing code to work unchanged on the new representation, though it is also possible to produce optimised code which works directly on the compact format without expanding it.

For example, a string such as *"abcdefg"*, whose value is known at compile time, might be represented with a length and a pointer into a static data area as follows:

The code for *String* produces a standard representation from this non-standard one by creating a *Cons* node which points to a *Char* node for the first character and a new *String* node representing the remaining characters. Existing polymorphic code for finding the length of a list, say, would work by expanding the string into a linked list of *Cons* nodes. Code could be added to handle the special case of *String* nodes simply by returning the length stored in the node itself.

A similar technique can be used for dynamically created structures. For example, once a string value has been fully evaluated as a chain of *Cons* and *Char* nodes, it can be compressed into the compact form shown above by the garbage collector. The compact form is regarded as the permanent storage representation, while the *Cons* and *Char* nodes are regarded as temporary storage for the parts of the string while it is being processed.

## 7.2.2 Functions

The code for a function head-evaluates its result expression and returns it to the caller. The arguments to the function are pointers to heap nodes, and are placed on top of the stack before the function is called. If the stack is pictured as growing downwards in memory from high locations to low ones, a common arrangement, then just before the code for a function *f* is entered to evaluate an application *f x y z*, the stack looks like this:

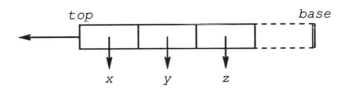

As an example of the kind of code generated for functions, the functions *id*, *cons* and *reverse*, defined by:

```
id x    =   x
cons x rxs   =   x : rxs
reverse xs   =   move xs []
```

might have the following code generated for them:

```
FUNCTION id     FUNCTION cons        FUNCTION reverse
    pop x           pop x rxs            pop xs
    enter x         new node             push nil xs
                    fill Cons x rxs      jump move
                    return 1
```

A function first pops its arguments off the stack with a *pop* instruction, and then evaluates its result. In a real assembly language, the variables *x*, *rxs* etc. would have to be given names which could not clash with global names such as those of entry points. In any case, register optimisation techniques would allow most of the variables to be held in registers rather than memory locations.

The *id* function illustrates the case when the result is an already existing node. The node is entered with an *enter* instruction which sets the *node* register and jumps to the associated code. When this code returns, it returns to the caller of the *id* function.

The *cons* function shows what happens when the result is an application of a built-in function or constructor. In-line code is generated to evaluate the result and return it to the caller. The *new* instruction sets the *node* register to the first free location in the heap, and the *fill* instruction fills in the contents of the new node.

In the case of the *reverse* function, the result is an application of another function *move* defined by the programmer. The code pushes the arguments for the *move* function onto the stack (in reverse order) and then uses a *jump* instruction to jump to the code for *move*, which eventually returns to the caller of the *reverse* function. The name *nil* represents a pointer to a single shared *Nil* node in the heap – representing a constant in this way avoids the need to create a new node each time it is needed. Register optimisation techniques would allow the *pop* and *push* instructions in a code block such as this to be combined into a more efficient sequence of instructions to adjust the stack as appropriate just before a jump or call.

The use of jumps rather than calls, where possible, leads to a situation in which, once a call is made to start the evaluation of a node, the flow of control is carried out by a series of jumps until the node becomes evaluated. At this point a single return instruction takes the flow of control directly back to the original caller. The use of jumps also allows many simple recursive functions to be compiled into loops.

If a function is passed as an argument or stored in a data structure, a node has to be created in the heap to represent it. When the function represented by the node is eventually applied to some arguments, the function is called by entering the node. A function such as *reverse* can be represented simply as a one-word node whose label points to the code for *reverse* shown above.

In the case of a built-in function or constructor for which in-line code is usually generated, an explicit function has to be provided. For example, if the : constructor is passed as an argument, it can be represented as a one-word node whose label points to the code for the *cons* function shown above.

If a partial application such as *(subtract 1)*, which represents a decrement function, is passed as an argument, then a block of code can be created for it during compilation of the expression in which it appears:

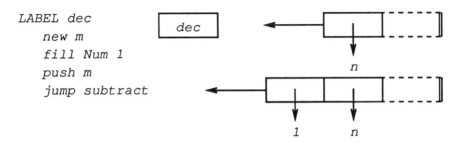

```
LABEL dec
    new m
    fill Num 1
    push m
    jump subtract
```

The picture shows the one-word node and its associated code, and also the state of the stack before and after the code is executed. The code for the partial application is entered when it is applied to an argument *n*, say. The code pushes the value *1* onto the stack and jumps to the code for *subtract* which then finds both its arguments on the stack.

A partial application may contain variables whose values are not known at compile time. Any such variables must be stored in the node so that they are accessible by its code. For example, suppose a function *sub* is defined which subtracts a given number *m* from each member of a list *ns*:

$$sub\ m\ ns\ =\ map\ (subtract\ m)\ ns$$

The code for the *sub* function must create a node representing the partial application *(subtract m)* to pass as an argument to *map*. The node contains the variable value *m*:

```
LABEL decm
    push node[1]
    jump subtract
```

As before, when the partial application is called, there will be an argument on the stack. The code copies *m* from the node onto the stack and jumps to `subtract`, which then finds both its arguments on the stack.

### 7.2.3   Suspensions

When an expression such as `f x` is evaluated, the argument `x` is pushed onto the stack and the code for `f` is entered. However, if evaluation of the expression has to be delayed, the expression must be stored as a heap node instead. These unevaluated expression nodes are often called **suspensions** or **closures**. For example, the `iterate` function is defined by:

$$iterate\ f\ x\ \ =\ \ x\ :\ iterate\ f\ (f\ x)$$

Since the expression `f x` on the right hand side is not necessarily going to be evaluated, the code for `iterate` must create a suspension node for it to pass as an argument in the recursive call. Moreover, since the node may be shared, arrangements must be made to overwrite it once it becomes evaluated. As `f` and `x` are both variables, they must both be stored in the node:

```
LABEL fx
    push node overwr
    push node[2]
    enter node[1]
```

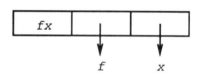

The code pushes a pointer to the node and the address of an entry point for overwriting it onto the stack. It then pushes `x` and enters `f`. The code for `f` creates a new node representing the value of `f x` and then returns to the `overwr` entry point. The `overwr` code pops the pointer to the old node off the stack and carries out the overwriting, as described in Section 7.3.2.

If a compound subexpression is suspended, it is not represented as a collection of interconnected nodes, but rather as a single node for which the associated code creates the other nodes as required. For example, if the expression `f (g 2)` is suspended, assuming that `f` and `g` are argument parameters, it is represented as:

```
LABEL fg2
    push node overwr
    new x
    fill g2 node[2]
    push x
    enter node[1]
```

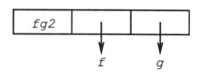

The code pushes the node and the *overwr* entry point onto the stack in order to arrange for overwriting, as described in Section 7.3.2. It then creates a new suspension node with label *g2* representing the argument to the function *f*. It then enters the node for *f*, which corresponds to jumping to the function which *f* represents. A separate but similar code block, not shown here, would be generated for the label *g2*. This would in turn arrange for its own overwriting, create a node representing *2* and enter the node representing the function *g*.

Strictness analysis can be used to reduce the need to create suspension nodes. If a subexpression such as *f x* is passed to a function which is known to be strict in that argument, then *f x* can be evaluated before the call rather than being suspended.

Analysis of reuse can be used to reduce the need to overwrite nodes. If it is known that there will only ever be one reference to a node, then the node need not be overwritten with its evaluated form, since it will never be used again.

## 7.3 Evaluation

In this section, the details of the flow of control in the G-machine are described. This includes the mechanisms for calling and returning, for overwriting suspension nodes once they become evaluated, and for carrying out input and output.

### 7.3.1 Calling

If a function is strict in an argument, then it needs to evaluate that argument before processing it. In particular, any argument on which pattern matching is used needs to be evaluated. A simple pattern match (see Section 6.4.4) can be compiled directly into code which evaluates the argument and then performs a switch on the tag value returned. For example, a function *empty* which tests whether a list is empty can be defined by:

```
empty []     =  True
empty (x:rxs)  =  False
```

The code generated for the *empty* function consists of code to enter its argument in order to evaluate it. This returns to a *CONTINUE* entry point which uses the tag value to switch to one of two *CASE* entry points:

```
FUNCTION empty
    pop xs
    push empty1
    enter xs

CONTINUE empty1
    switch empty2 empty3
CASE empty2
    setnode true
    return 1
CASE empty3
    setnode false
    return 0
```

The code for *empty* pops its argument, pushes the return address *empty1* onto the stack and then enters the argument node *xs* with an *enter* instruction to evaluate it. When the evaluation is complete, control returns to the continuation entry point *empty1*. This uses a *switch* instruction to jump to either *empty2* or *empty3* according to the tag value returned from the evaluation. A *setnode* instruction is then used to set the *node* register to a pointer to a shared node representing *True* or one representing *False*, and a suitable tag value is returned to the caller of the *empty* function.

When a call is made, the return address and any values stored with it form a **stack frame**. At any one time, the stack contains a mixture of function arguments and stack frames. As the stack grows downwards in memory, a stack frame looks just like a heap node, with the return address corresponding to a label. The size and layout of a stack frame needs to be available for memory management purposes and, as with heap nodes, this information can be stored just before the continuation point in the code pointed to by the return address.

For this reason, the continuation point does not directly follow the call, hence the need for explicit handling of the return address rather than using a normal call instruction. In fact this scheme allows considerable flexibility – any continuation point can be chosen for return after a call.

As an example of saving values in stack frames during calls, consider the *times* function defined by:

```
times m n  =  m * n
```

The code generated for this function might be:

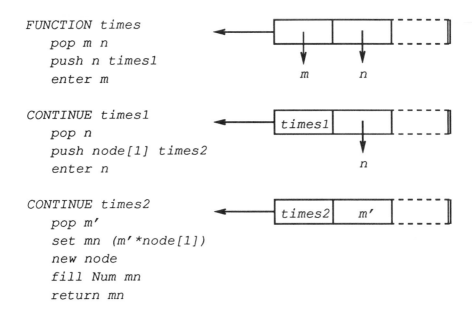

```
FUNCTION times
    pop m n
    push n times1
    enter m

CONTINUE times1
    pop n
    push node[1] times2
    enter n

CONTINUE times2
    pop m'
    set mn (m'*node[1])
    new node
    fill Num mn
    return mn
```

When the function is entered, the stack contains the arguments. During the first call to evaluate *m*, a two-node stack frame is used to store the return address *times1* and the node representing *n*. During the second call, the stack frame is used to save the raw integer *m'* representing the value of *m*.

In an optimising compiler, the fact that this function is strict in both arguments can be used to evaluate the arguments before the function is called. The function could then take its arguments and return its result as raw integers held in registers. Indeed, the whole function can be replaced in-line wherever it is called. However, if a node representing *times* (or a partial application of it) is created to be passed as an argument to some other function, then the above code which evaluates the arguments is still needed. Moreover, if the operator * is passed as an argument, then the above code can be used to represent it.

## 7.3.2 Overwriting

The overwriting of a suspension node occurs after the node is evaluated. To achieve this, the code associated with the node does a call to evaluate the node and then overwrites the original node with the result.

To avoid problems with nodes being of different sizes, and to cope with the fact that we may want to overwrite a node with another which already exists, without making an unnecessary copy, the old node is replaced by an **indirection** node which contains the label *Ind* and a pointer to the new node. As an *Ind* node is two words long, any suspension node which is to be overwritten must have at least two words:

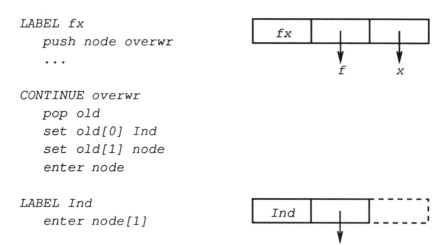

```
    LABEL fx
        push node overwr
        ...

    CONTINUE overwr
        pop old
        set old[0] Ind
        set old[1] node
        enter node

    LABEL Ind
        enter node[1]
```

The code associated with the suspension node makes a call to evaluate the node by pushing a frame on the stack consisting of the *overwr* return address and a pointer to the node. Since the overwriting code is the same for all nodes, there need only be a single *overwr* code block shared by all suspension nodes.

The *overwr* code fills the first two words of the old node with an indirection node which points to the new version of the node returned from the evaluation. The code for *Ind* simply jumps to the code for the node it points to.

The new node is then entered. If the new node represents a data value, then the tag register already contains a suitable tag, and so the *enter* instruction is correct but unnecessary – a simple *return* would do. However, the new node may represent a function value, in which case entering it causes the function to be applied to the arguments currently on the stack.

There is a subtle problem with this overwriting mechanism in the case when the suspension node represents a function value. When an expression representing a function is evaluated, it is not normally returned as a result node, but rather applied to some arguments on the stack.

For example, consider the call *map (\*) [2,3,4]* which produces the list of functions *[(2\*), (3\*), (4\*)]*. The code for the *map* function creates a suspension node with associated entry point *fx*, say, containing the *times* entry point and a pointer to a node representing *2* to represent the first member *(2\*)* of the result. When this is eventually applied to an argument *21*, say, the stack does not have the right form:

```
LABEL fx
    push node overwr
    push node[2]
    enter node[1]
```

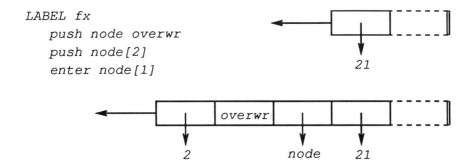

When the code for *times* is entered, a two-word stack frame appears between the two arguments which *times* expects. To solve this problem, code can be inserted just after the *times* entry point, and the entry point to every function, to check for this situation.

One way to do the checking is to test the top words on the stack to see if they are pointers to heap nodes, and thus genuine arguments. Alternatively, a special frame register can be used which points to the latest stack frame, and the current top of the stack can be compared with this. Such a frame register is often used in implementations of procedural languages – each time a call is made, the previous value of the frame register is stored in the new stack frame and then restored when the call returns.

If a stack frame is found, it contains an old node which needs overwriting. Its new value is a partial application of the function just entered to the arguments which have been placed on the stack since the stack frame was put there. In the above example, the code for *times*, on encountering the stack frame, pops *2* off the stack, creates a node representing *(2\*)* and returns. Control passes to the *overwr* entry point which overwrites the old node with the new one and then enters the new node. This causes *times* to be entered for a second time, this time with both arguments as they should be on the stack, and so evaluation continues normally.

### 7.3.3 Input and Output

Input and output involve interaction with the operating system which is (usually) procedural, so they have to be implemented using side-effects. As an example of handling input, consider the implementation of the standard input *$-* representing the stream of characters typed on the keyboard.

This can be represented by a node with a label *Stdin* and two further unused words to allow it to be overwritten directly by a *Cons* node when it is evaluated. When the program starts, there must only be one *Stdin* node stored in the heap, shared by all references to *$-*. Evaluation of this node causes it to be overwritten with a *Cons* node which points to a node representing the first character from the keyboard, and to a new *Stdin* node representing the remaining characters:

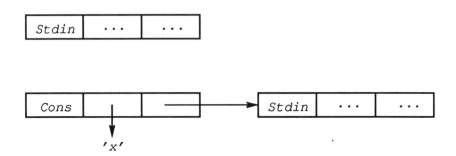

To cope with output, the result expression can be passed to a procedure *print* which evaluates and prints out the members of a character stream one by one. If the result expression is not of type *[char]*, then a *show* function must be applied to it first. For example, if the result expression is *42*, then the procedure call *print (shownum 42)* is made.

The *print* procedure head-evaluates its argument list, then evaluates the first member, i.e. the first character, prints the character, and then loops to process the tail of its argument list.

## 7.4   Memory Management

Memory management involves detecting when the stack or the heap runs out of space. If the stack space runs out, more space is allocated for it, if possible. If the heap space runs out, then a **garbage collection** is carried out to reclaim space taken up by nodes which are no longer in use.

To detect when space runs out, it may be possible to put the stack and heap in separate memory segments and to rely on the computer's own memory management hardware to detect when attempts are made to access memory locations beyond the boundaries. Otherwise, each entry point in the code must begin with checks to see if there is sufficient space left. One possible arrangement can be pictured as:

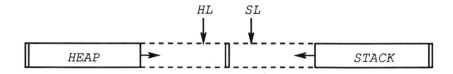

The available memory space is divided into the heap, which grows forwards from the beginning, and the stack, which grows backwards from the end. This allows either space to be extended at the expense of the other.

Memory is allocated on the heap simply by moving the top of the heap forward, and nothing is deleted until a garbage collection takes place. This means that a single heap overflow test can be used to cover all the nodes allocated in a code block, rather than one test for each node. Also, the relative positions of the nodes allocated in a code block are known at compile time, and it is easy to generate efficient code to fill in a pointer from one node to another, even if the second node is allocated later.

A heap limit register *HL* can be used to speed up heap overflow checks. It points some fixed distance, say 100 words, from the end of the available heap space. For any code block which allocates less than 100 words of heap, a simple comparison between the top of the heap and *HL* suffices. Stack checks can be carried out in a similar way with a stack limit register *SL*.

No checks need be carried out at *CASE* entry points, since they can be incorporated into the checks for the block containing the relevant *switch* instruction – these can check that there is sufficient space to cover any of the cases. It may also be possible to incorporate the stack overflow check for a *CONTINUE* entry point into the check for the block containing the relevant call, since the position of the top of the stack is preserved across calls.

The heap handles a high turnover of small, variable sized nodes. Heap space tends to be used up very quickly, and so an efficient garbage collector is needed. The job of the garbage collector is to find the **live** nodes, i.e. those which are still in use, and to move them together so that there are no gaps. All the space that was taken up by **dead** nodes, ones which are no longer active, can then be made available for subsequent use. The live nodes are all those which are pointed to by registers or by words in the stack, together with all the nodes to which they point, directly or indirectly.

In order to move heap nodes, the garbage collector needs to know the size and layout of each node. The layout specifies which words in the node are pointers to other nodes – such pointers need to be updated to point to the new positions of the other nodes. The size and layout information can be stored just before the entry point in the code to which the node label points. For efficiency, they can be stored in the form of pointers to blocks of code which are optimised to handle the garbage collection of nodes of each particular size and layout.

The stack is a mixture of function arguments, which are pointers to heap nodes, and stack frames. To scan the stack and find out which words in it are pointers to heap nodes, the collector needs to recognise the return address at the start of a stack frame, which it can do by testing to see if it is a pointer into the code rather than the heap, and then use the size and layout of the stack frame to find the node pointers within it. This size and layout information is available through the return address in exactly the same way as the size and layout of a node is available through its label.

One of the simplest and most efficient techniques for moving and updating the live nodes is to use a **copying** garbage collector. With this technique, a second heap space is used and the live nodes are copied from the old one to the new one. As each live node is found and copied, a "forwarding address" is left in the old heap which points from the old node to its new position in the new heap. Once the nodes pointed to by registers and the stack have been copied, the nodes in the new heap are scanned in order to find more live nodes, which are copied across as they are found, and to update the pointers. The part of the new heap containing nodes which have been copied but not yet updated acts as a queue of work still to be done – when it becomes empty, all the live nodes have been found, copied and updated. Details of the method can be found in Field & Harrison[6].

One of the advantages of this method of garbage collection is that only live cells are accessed. In typical programs, the heap grows linearly with the time spent processing, whereas the number of live cells grows much more slowly, if at all. Thus the percentage of time spent garbage collecting is proportional to the percentage of live cells just before a garbage collection. This percentage can be made arbitrarily small by providing more memory, and thus increasing the time between garbage collections.

The copying technique is suitable when there is plenty of memory space available, or when the computer supports virtual memory. A similar garbage collection technique which uses only one heap space, and so is suitable when less memory is available, is described in a paper by Jonkers[8].

## 7.5   Exercises

1. Show how the evaluation of the expression *repeat 1* would proceed with simple graph reduction, as described in Section 7.1, using either of the definitions of *repeat* given in Appendix B. Which definition is more efficient?

2. Show the G-machine code which would be generated for the standard *until* function. Is the result a procedural loop, i.e. a block of code which does not use up stack space as it runs? What kind of function definitions get compiled into procedural loops?

3. Demonstrate how the G-machine evaluation mechanism is able to evaluate $- ++ $- without reading in the standard input twice.

4. Extend the assembly language described in this chapter to cover all aspects of functional language implementation. Write a prototype translator to convert this assembly language into a procedural language of your choice, thus providing a prototype implementation mechanism.

# Chapter 8

# The Meaning of Programs

It is necessary to give a precise meaning to programs if you want to investigate and predict their behaviour, transform them in ways which preserve their meaning, or prove that they are correct. The study of the meaning of programs is called **semantics**. The theory of semantics can also be used to investigate properties of compilers, and even to prove them correct.

Programs are given meanings in two different ways. A **declarative** meaning is one in which a program is regarded as a static definition of values and algorithms. Mathematical interpretations are given for all the features of the language so that properties of programs can be investigated independently of any particular implementation method. An **operational** meaning for a program is a precise description of the way in which a program is executed. Implementation principles are laid down for the language so that the behaviour of programs can be predicted.

The declarative meaning of a functional program is usually given by specifying a set of mathematical values, and then describing what values are represented by the expressions and definitions in the program. This kind of semantics is called **denotational** semantics, because it focuses on the values which program features denote. This contrasts with logic programming languages which are usually given a declarative semantics in terms of logical deduction from facts and rules, but the aim is the same – to provide a way of reading a program as a static definition of the results it produces.

The operational meaning of a functional program is usually given in terms of reduction as described in Section 2.6. This is usually studied in the context of the lambda calculus, a minimal functional language often used in theoretical studies which is described briefly in Chapter 9. Again, this contrasts with the operational semantics of logic programming languages, which is usually presented in terms of goals, searching and backtracking.

In this chapter, we first describe the special relationship which exists in functional languages between these two different views of the meaning of programs. The remainder of the chapter is devoted to a description of the set of values needed to provide a denotational semantics for functional languages.

## 8.1   Values and Behaviours

The most important property of the semantics of a pure functional language is that the declarative and operational views of the language coincide exactly, in the following way:

> Every expression denotes a value, and there are values corresponding to all possible program behaviours. The behaviour produced by an expression in any context is completely determined by its value, and vice versa.

This principle, which is usually rather opaquely called **referential transparency**, can also be pictured in the following way:

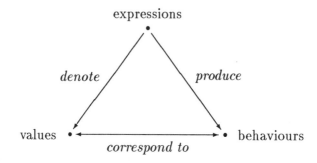

It is this principle which ensures that mathematical properties of programs are also real properties of their practical behaviour. This not only makes the mathematical study of programs easier, it also helps programmers, consciously or otherwise, to gain a unified and consistent understanding of the language.

The principle has many consequences. In particular, an expression has no effect other than that determined by its value. The value of an expression depends only on the values of its variables and subexpressions. Expressions with equal values are interchangeable. The evaluation mechanism corresponds exactly to converting an expression into its value.

This contrasts with almost all other languages. In other languages, including procedural and logic programming languages, this exact correspondence between the declarative and operational views is usually only true of a subset of the language not normally regarded as sufficient for practical programming, or else the declarative semantics has to be made so complicated and obscure that it is really just an operational semantics in disguise.

To achieve this correspondence between the two different views of the meaning of programs, we need values to represent lazy behaviour and higher-order functions, as well as the usual kinds of mathematical values. The set of values which is needed forms a special mathematical structure called a **domain**. The theory of domains is described in the book by Schmidt [12]. Rather than study the theory of domains in detail, we will describe informally the values needed to specify the semantics of a functional language such as Miranda, and the relationships between those values.

To simplify matters, we will ignore restrictions imposed on the set of values by types or type checking. It is as if the language has a single type to which all values belong, and values are distinguishable only by their constructors at run time. The type system can then be regarded as an extra feature which rejects certain programs at compile time, mostly ones which would otherwise produce errors at run time.

The set of values can be divided into data values and function values, into finite and infinite values, and into total and partial values. This gives us eight possible categories from total finite data values to partial infinite function values. We will first look at finite data values, including partial ones, then at infinite data values, then at function values.

## 8.2 Finite Data Values

The value of an expression representing finite data is simply the fully evaluated form of that expression, i.e. an equivalent expression built up from constants and constructors.

To be more precise, every total finite data value has a unique representation as an expression built up using only constants and constructors, and in which each constructor is applied to the right number of arguments (no partial applications). Logic programmers would call these "ground terms". For example, if we define a new type representing binary trees of numbers:

```
trees   ::=   Empty | Fork trees num trees
```

then the values which are introduced are all the expressions which are built up from *Empty*, *Fork* and numbers:

```
Empty
Fork Empty 1 Empty
Fork (Fork Empty 2 Empty) 5 Empty
. . . .
```

The built-in types can be described in the same way. Booleans and characters are enumerated types. Restricted integers can also be regarded as enumerated, but unrestricted integers or floating point numbers are structured types whose representation is hidden. Tuples can be regarded as being built with a sequence of constructors called *Pair*, *Triple*, ..., say. Lists are built from the constant *[]* and constructor *:*, and so the values of lists can be represented using these. For example, we will say that the value of *[1,2,3]* is *1:2:3:[]* . In this way, built-in types too can all be regarded as being built up from constants and constructors.

In order to take account of laziness, interactive behaviour and so on, we have to introduce **partial** data values. One of the simplest programs you can write is:

```
x  =  x
```

In operational terms, the equation specifies that in order to calculate *x*, you must calculate *x*. If you try to evaluate *x*, the program will get caught in an infinite loop, and you will have to interrupt it. A compiler could be made to detect this particular simple kind of infinite loop, but it cannot be made to detect all infinite loops. That would be equivalent to solving the infamous **halting problem**: this is the problem of determining whether a given program will ever halt (terminate), and it has been proven that there is no algorithm for solving this for arbitrary programs. As an illustration, nobody (yet) knows whether the following function terminates for all possible integer arguments, or whether there is some large integer *n* which causes an infinite loop:

```
f n
=  0,              if n <= 1
=  f (n div 2),    if n mod 2 = 0
=  f (3*n + 1),    otherwise
```

Thus, we have to accept that there are programs which compile, but which fail to terminate at run time. In order to preserve the correspondence between declarative and operational meanings, there must be mathematical values to represent this kind of program behaviour.

The mathematical symbol ⊥, which is called **bottom**, is introduced to represent the value of any program which gets into an infinite loop without producing any output. The value ⊥ is sometimes called "undefined", but for us it is a perfectly well defined value – it is just that trying to evaluate it may take a long time. Note that ⊥ is regarded as finite, mathematically, even though it takes an "infinite" amount of time to compute. In Miranda examples, we will use an identifier *bottom* with value ⊥, defined by:

```
bottom  =  bottom
```

You can think of ⊥ as an error value, since a program with this value is presumably not doing what you intended, but it is an error which the run time system cannot catch and report. Explicit error values such as those generated by the *error* function, or by run time argument checks for built-in functions, are usually given the value ⊥ too, even though they do not have exactly the same behaviour as an infinite loop. The semantics could be extended to cover such error messages, but it is not worth the extra complication, since we are mostly interested in correct programs rather than ones which produce errors. If the language contained an exception handling mechanism in which errors could be caught and dealt with by the program itself, then such an extension to the semantics would become necessary.

The value ⊥ is the simplest partial data value. Other partial data values are ones containing infinite loops as substructures. For example, consider the expression *[42, bottom]*. If you try to evaluate it, it will never terminate. However, it does print out something before getting into an infinite loop and, in some contexts, information can be extracted from the expression without causing an infinite loop:

```
? [42,bottom]          (This example fails to terminate
[42,                    and has to be interrupted.)

? hd [42,bottom]
42

? # [42,bottom]
2
```

This means that *[42,bottom]* has a different behaviour from *bottom*, and so must have a different value. Every part of the expression, except for *bottom*, can be tested and accessed. Thus the expression *[42,bottom]* is said to have the value *42:⊥:[]*.

All partial data values have unique mathematical representations in exactly the same way as total data values, except that the symbol ⊥ is allowed as an extra "honorary constant". Evaluation of a partial data value only gets stuck in an infinite loop if a substructure with value ⊥ is evaluated.

Partial data values are important in the description of interactive behaviour. For example, here are two possible definitions of a function which squares each number in a list of numbers:

```
squares ns  =  [n^2 | n <- ns]


squares' ns
  =  [],                  if #ns = 0
  =  [n^2 | n <- ns],    otherwise
```

The two definitions appear equivalent. For example, if you apply them to *[1,2,3]*, you get *[1,4,9]* in both cases. However, if these definitions are used as part of an interactive program which repeatedly reads in a number and prints out its square, the second function does not interleave the input and output properly – it waits until all the numbers are typed in before printing any of the answers.

Consider the value *1:2:3:*⊥. It cannot be written using the square bracket notation, because it does not have a well-defined length, or rather it has length ⊥. This value can be taken to represent a situation in which the numbers *1*, *2* and *3* have been typed in, and the user is waiting to see what happens before typing any more in. In fact if the user were never to type anything in again, the value input would be exactly *1:2:3:*⊥. When given this input, a correct interactive program would print out the answers to all three questions, and then wait for more input, i.e. it would print out the value *1:4:9:*⊥. We can use this to test the above function definitions. When applied to the value *1:2:3:*⊥, the *squares* function returns the value *1:4:9:*⊥ whereas *squares'* does not. Of the two, only *squares* is suitable for interactive purposes:

```
? squares (1:2:3:bottom)
[1,4,9                            (Fails to terminate.)


? squares' (1:2:3:bottom)
[                                 (Fails to terminate.)
```

In general, we can differentiate between functions with different interactive behaviour by saying that they return different results when applied to partial data values, i.e. they are different functions.

## 8.3   Infinite Data Values

Infinite values can only be manipulated in a computer by producing better and better finite **approximations** to them as required. Mathematically, it is extremely convenient to use partial values, not only as values in their own right, but also as a way of representing finite approximations to infinite values.

One way to look at it is this. Previously, we took the value $1:2:3:\perp$ to represent the situation in which a user has typed in $1$, $2$ and $3$, and is waiting to see what happens. When the user finally types more numbers in, the value "becomes" some longer list $1:2:3:4:\ldots$, say, so it makes sense to regard $1:2:3:\perp$ as an approximation to $1:2:3:4:\ldots$

Another way of looking at it is to regard $\perp$ as representing a value about which we have no information. Then $1:2:3:\perp$ represents a value about which we know some information, the first three members, but no more. With this new interpretation of $\perp$, it is again sensible to regard $1:2:3:\perp$ as an approximation to any longer list $1:2:3:4:\ldots$, because they are the same except that we have more information about the latter.

Operationally, an infinite value like $[1..]$ is represented at any particular moment by an expression such as $1:2:3:[4..]$ consisting of a finite data structure with an embedded unevaluated expression $[4..]$. The value $1:2:3:\perp$ can be regarded as representing all the information which can be extracted from the expression $1:2:3:[4..]$ without further evaluation. In this way, the history of evaluation of the expression $[1..]$ corresponds directly to a sequence of better and better finite approximations.

We write $x \sqsubseteq y$ to mean "value $x$ is an approximation to value $y$". The $\sqsubseteq$ symbol is a square less-than-or-equals sign. We can also use the symbol $\sqsubset$ to mean "an approximation to, but not equal to". If $x$ and $y$ are data values, then $x$ is an approximation to $y$ if $x$ is the same as $y$, except that some of the embedded subexpressions are replaced by $\perp$. For example:

$$1:\perp:3:\perp \quad \sqsubseteq \quad 1:2:3:\perp \quad \sqsubseteq \quad 1:2:3:[]$$

The value $\perp$ itself is an approximation to all other values. The value $True:[]$ has the 5 approximations $\perp$, $\perp:\perp$, $True:\perp$, $\perp:[]$, and itself.

An infinite data value is the limit of an increasing sequence of partial finite data values, each of which is an approximation to the next. For example the infinite list $[1..]$ is the limit of the following sequence of approximations:

$$\perp \quad \sqsubset \quad 1:\perp \quad \sqsubset \quad 1:2:\perp \quad \sqsubset \quad 1:2:3:\perp \quad \sqsubset \quad \ldots$$

All infinite data values are limits of this kind. Each infinite data value has a unique mathematical representation as an infinite expression built up from the constants and constructors as before. Thus, the infinite list *[1..]* has the unique infinite representation *1:2:3:4:5:...*, though of course only a finite approximation to it can exist at any one time during the running of a program.

Infinite data values can only be defined indirectly in programs using recursive definitions. The expression *[1..]*, for example, is an abbreviation for *from 1* where the function *from* is defined recursively as:

```
from n  =  n : from (n+1)
```

Thus the list is represented at run-time as *from 1*, then as *1:(from 2)*, then *1:2:(from 3)* and so on. The information which can be extracted from these expressions corresponds to the approximations discussed above.

There are partial infinite values such as $\perp:\perp:\perp:...$, as well as total infinite values. These are limits of sequences of finite approximations in just the same way. It is also possible to form increasing sequences of these partial infinite values, and these too have limits. However, these limits are infinite values of the same form as we have been discussing, and they have finite approximations as well as infinite ones.

We have now described all the non-function values. To summarise, they are all the expressions, finite or infinite, made up from a given set of constants and constructors, and the symbol $\perp$.

## 8.4   Function Values

Finding a suitable mathematical way of specifying function values is rather difficult. Before presenting a method which works, we will discuss two methods which do not work.

We have seen that each data value has a unique representation as a finite or infinite structure, and that evaluation of an expression is essentially a conversion into that representation. Unfortunately, there is no way of converting an expression representing a function into a unique form. If there were, there would be a general way of telling whether two different definitions such as

```
f []      =  []
f (x:rxs)  =  x:rxs
```

```
f' []     =   []
f' (x:rxs)   =   x : (f' rxs)
```

define the same function. In this case they do, since they both return the same results on all possible arguments – they are both the identity on lists. However, if this could be decided automatically for all pairs of definitions, it would provide a way of solving the unsolvable halting problem.

The impossibility of finding a unique computable representation for functions has practical implications for the design of functional languages. It means that functions cannot have their representations examined, e.g. they cannot be read in, printed out, or compared with each other, otherwise different representations of the same function value could be made to produce different behaviours. This would go against the principle of referential transparency described at the beginning of the chapter. Functions have to be treated like an abstract data type in which application is the only operation provided.

A second possibility for specifying function values would be to use a convention which is common in mathematics, which is to regard a function as a set of pairs. Each pair contains an argument and corresponding result. For example the value of the squaring function $(^2)$ would be the set of pairs $\{ (1,1), (2,4), (3,9), \ldots \}$. However, the way in which higher-order functions are used in functional languages makes this approach impossible too. The problem is that the set of function values required is highly recursive.

For example, the standard identity function $id$ can be applied to itself, with $id\ id$ having the value $id$. If functions were specified as sets of pairs, the pair $(id, id)$ would belong to the set of pairs $id$, which is impossible because no set is allowed to belong to itself, directly or indirectly. Moreover, the complete set of values $V$ would have to include the set $V \to V$ of all functions from $V$ to $V$ which is a bigger set than $V$ itself.

The solution to these problems is to consider only computable functions rather than all possible functions, and to specify a function as the limit of a sequence of finite approximations, as we did for infinite data values.

Computable functions can only produce results for partial arguments by using their well-defined parts, and for infinite arguments by using their successive finite approximations. Thus computable functions must be **continuous**, i.e. they must preserve the notions of approximation and limit. The definition of continuity is:

$$\begin{array}{llllllll}
\textbf{if} & a & \sqsubseteq & b & \sqsubseteq & c & \sqsubseteq & \ldots & \text{tends to} & z \\
\textbf{then} & f\ a & \sqsubseteq & f\ b & \sqsubseteq & f\ c & \sqsubseteq & \ldots & \text{tends to} & f\ z
\end{array}$$

For example, if we apply the function *squares* defined in Section 8.2 to a sequence of partial approximations tending to *[1..]* , we get:

```
⊥  ⊑  1:⊥  ⊑  1:2:⊥  ⊑  ...   tends to 1:2:3:4:...
⊥  ⊑  1:⊥  ⊑  1:4:⊥  ⊑  ...   tends to 1:4:9:16:...
```

Technically, the continuous functions still include some non-computable functions as well as all the computable ones, but continuity is a simple and natural mathematical restriction, and is sufficient for what follows.

To define functions as limits of finite approximations, we must specify when a function is finite, when one function is an approximation to another, and when a function is the limit of a sequence of functions.

The value ⊥, as well as being an approximation to all data values, is also an approximation to all functions. However, it is not regarded as a function itself. The most approximate function, which is an approximation to all other functions, is the one which returns ⊥ on all arguments, i.e. the function defined by:

```
f x  =  bottom
```

This is the simplest finite function. More generally, a function is finite if it can be specified by giving finite results for it on a finite number of finite arguments, and then extending it in a minimal (most approximate) continuous way to all other values. For example the value of the function *f* defined by:

```
f []  =  []
f (True:bs)   =  [1]
f (False:bs)  =  2:bottom
```

is finite, because it can be specified by saying that it takes *[]* to *[]* and *True:⊥* to *1:[]* and *False:⊥* to *2:⊥*. The minimal extension gives the result ⊥ (actually a type error) on all values except lists of booleans. It also gives result ⊥ on any non-empty list with first member ⊥. By continuity, it must give result *1:[]* on any value which is approximated by *True:⊥*, i.e. any list with first member *True*. Finally, it must give a result of *2:⊥* on any argument approximated by *False:⊥*, i.e. any list with first member *False*.

One function *f* is an approximation to another function *g* if the results produced by *f* are approximations to those produced by *g*. Similarly, the limit of a sequence of functions is the function which produces the limits of the result values. All infinite functions are limits of sequences of finite functions in this way. These rules can be summarised as:

$$f \quad \sqsubseteq \quad g \qquad \textbf{means}$$
$$f \ x \ \sqsubseteq \ g \ x \qquad \textbf{for all } x$$

$$g \quad \sqsubseteq \ h \quad \sqsubseteq \ \ldots \qquad \qquad \textbf{tends to} \quad f \qquad \textbf{means}$$
$$g \ x \ \sqsubseteq \ h \ x \ \sqsubseteq \ \ldots \qquad \textbf{tends to} \quad f \ x \qquad \textbf{for all } x$$

It is now possible to illustrate the way in which a function definition specifies a function value as a sequence of finite approximations. As an example, we will use the factorial function `fac`. For simplicity, we choose a one-line definition using the `test` function:

```
fac n  =  test (n=0) 1 (n*fac(n-1))
```

The first approximation to `fac` is the function which always returns $\bot$. At each stage, the next approximation is obtained by substituting the current one into the result expression of the equation:

```
f0 n  =  bottom
f1 n  =  test (n=0) 1 (n*f0(n-1))
f2 n  =  test (n=0) 1 (n*f1(n-1))
f3 n  =  test (n=0) 1 (n*f2(n-1))
f4 n  =  test (n=0) 1 (n*f3(n-1))
  ...
```

Each of these functions is finite – `f1` returns the right result for argument `0` and $\bot$ for all other arguments, `f2` returns the results for arguments `0` and `1` only, `f3` returns the results for `0`, `1` and `2` only, and so on. This process defines an increasing sequence of finite functions with limit `fac`, which returns the right result on all natural number arguments, and $\bot$ for all other arguments.

The functions `f0`, `f1`, ...are closely related to the way in which the `fac` function is evaluated. Each step in the evaluation is equivalent to using the next function in the sequence:

```
?    fac 3              ↔    f0 3 = ⊥
→    3 * fac 2          ↔    f1 3 = 3*⊥ = ⊥
→    3 * 2 * fac 1      ↔    f2 3 = 3*2*⊥ = ⊥
→    3 * 2 * 1 * fac 0  ↔    f3 3 = 3*2*1*⊥ = ⊥
→    3 * 2 * 1 * 1      ↔    f4 3 = 3*2*1*1 = 6
```

In general, the approximations produced depends on the form of the definition, and they are not necessarily finite. Nevertheless, they can be very useful – a proof by induction on the sequence amounts to a proof by induction on the number of recursive calls made to the function.

## 8.5　Exercises

1. What value is defined by the equation:

   $$n \ = \ n + 1$$

   and what behaviour does it exhibit when you try to evaluate it?

2. Write down all the *11* approximations of the value *False:True:[]*.

3. Finite data values have a tree structure which can be represented as in Section 4.5. For example, the value in Question 2 can be represented by:

   ```
   value
   =  Tree "Cons" [Tree "False" [],
      Tree "Cons" [Tree "True" [],
      Tree "Nil" []]]
   ```

   Define a function in Miranda which takes an arbitrary tree and determines how many approximations a value with that structure would have. Check that the tree above gives the answer 11.

4. Define an expression which has value $\bot:\bot:\bot:\ldots$

5. The sequence of approximations to the *fac* function can be demonstrated by defining a function *nextfac* which takes one approximation to the next, i.e. *nextfac f0* gives *f1*, *nextfac f1* gives *f2* and so on. Write down a definition of *nextfac* of the form:

   ```
   nextfac f n  =  ....
   ```

   The function *fac* can then be defined as the limit of the sequence with the definition:

   ```
   fac n  =  nextfac fac n
   ```

   Verify that this version of the *fac* function produces the same results as the original by evaluating them both on a few example arguments.

6. Prove that the function *fac* gives the result $\bot$ on all negative numbers by showing that this is true of each of its approximations.

# Chapter 9

# Other Functional Languages

Many different functional languages have been defined, and in this chapter we look at just a few – those which are distinctive and which represent turning points in the development of the subject. They will only be described very briefly, with a minimum of detail, concentrating rather on the contributions they have made.

## 9.1   The Lambda Calculus

The lambda calculus is generally regarded as the first functional language. It was introduced in the 1930s as a tool for the mathematical investigation of computation. It is described briefly in many books on functional languages, and its theory is developed in R. Turner [18] and Barendregt [4].

Since the language is intended as a theoretical tool, it has a minimum of syntax. In the simplest version of the language, a program is a single expression, and there are only two constructs allowed. In the first of these, which gives the language its name, the Greek letter $\lambda$ (lambda) is used to represent function values. The second is function application as in Miranda. For example, the expressions:

```
λx.x
λf.λg.λx.f(g x)
```

represent the identity function and the composition function respectively. A lambda expression $\lambda x...$ can be read "the function which takes $x$ to ..." The only reduction rule necessary for evaluation is the application of a lambda expression to an argument:

$$? \quad (\lambda f.\lambda g.\lambda x.f(g\ x))\ (\lambda y.y)$$
$$\rightarrow \quad \lambda g.\lambda x.\ (\lambda y.y)\ (g\ x)$$

and evaluation ends when no more reduction steps are possible. No data values are necessary, as these can be represented using functions. Even recursion is not necessary – a recursive function can be represented as the limit of a sequence of finite approximations as in Section 8.4.

The lambda calculus is not suitable as a programming language because of its lack of features. Nevertheless, it is a very important language because it represents a 'lowest common denominator' for functional languages in which the theory of functions and their semantics and evaluation is usually carried out. The theory of more recent languages is often studied by relating them to the lambda calculus and using known results.

## 9.2   Lisp

Lisp arose in the 1950s out of the need for symbolic as opposed to numerical computation, and there are many dialects still in common use today, particularly for artificial intelligence applications. There are many books about Lisp, such as the one by Winston & Horn [20].

Some of the features of Lisp which have influenced later languages are: an emphasis on list processing, the ability for functions to be examined and new ones created, and the use of good interactive development environments. As an example, a definition of the factorial function in Lisp is:

```
(defun fac (n)
    (cond ((zerop n) 1)
          (t (times n (fac (sub1 n)))))))
```

Here, cond is a conditional function, zerop tests whether a number is zero, and so on. Thus the programming style used can often be very functional in nature. However, Lisp is a hybrid language, and much of its power comes from its procedural features – there are features for procedural assignment and update of both data and functions.

## 9.3   ML

The language ML, which stands for Meta Language, was developed in the 1970s as a general purpose functional language, initially used to support theorem proving. This was one of the first practical languages to emphasise the functional style rather than the procedural style, and it contains many important innovations, including the polymorphic type system used in most later functional languages. ML is one of the first functional languages for which optimising compilers have been developed and also one of the first to become standardised – see the book on Standard ML by Wikström [19].

In practice, the language is quite close to the Miranda style, though with different syntax conventions. For example, a function to find the length of a list can be written:

```
fun   len nil  =   0
  |   len (x :: rxs)   =   1 + len rxs
```

Here, the function definition is introduced with keyword *fun* and continued on a second line using the vertical bar symbol *|* .

The ML language is not purely functional. It provides procedural features involving side effects for performing input and output, for improving efficiency and for debugging. However, the language can be used very effectively in a pure functional style, keeping the use of the procedural features to a minimum.

Also, Standard ML is not lazy. This makes some of the styles of programming presented in this book rather harder to implement. If the evaluation of an expression needs to be delayed, this has to be programmed explicitly by representing the expression as a function of no arguments which returns the result of evaluating the expression when it is called.

## 9.4   Haskell

Miranda is representative of a large number of lazy, purely functional programming languages which have emerged recently, mainly for research purposes. These languages are all rather similar, with mostly syntactic differences. This proliferation was felt by the research community to be rather unhelpful and, at a conference in 1987, it was decided to consolidate the understanding and experience gained by designing a single, standard, non-proprietary, pure functional language, incorporating the popular features of these languages, and acting as a focus for implementation efforts and further language experiments. The result is a language called Haskell (named after the logician Haskell B. Curry). See the Haskell Report [21].

The Haskell language is somewhat larger and more comprehensive than Miranda, although they are very closely related. Almost all of the features of Miranda are available in Haskell in some form, though sometimes with a different syntax. Haskell also contains several features, some of them experimental, which are not found in Miranda.

There are several features of Haskell which the version of Miranda described in this book does not have, but which have been used successfully in other functional languages. For example, Haskell allows lambda expressions, similar to those of the lambda calculus described in Section 9.1, "as" patterns which allow names to be attached to arguments in a more general way when pattern matching, programmer defined infix operators, mutually recursive modules, arrays and an extended input and output system providing better interfacing with the operating system.

In addition, Haskell supports a "nested" style of programming in which many constructs such as guards, local definitions and patterns, are generalised so that they can be used inside subexpressions, and not just at the top level of definitions. For example, one can write:

```
abssqrt n    =   sqrt (if n<0 then -n else n)

abssqrt' n   =   sqrt (m where m = abs n)

scan op c xs  =   c : case xs of
    []  ->  []
    x:rxs  ->  scan op (c 'op' x) rxs
```

Here, 'op' is the equivalent of $op in Miranda.

This idea of allowing constructs to be embedded within expressions helps to make the language more expressive. In addition, it makes it easier to express program transformations such as those described in Chapter 6.

One of the main novel features of the Haskell language is the use of classes to provide a more structured and uniform approach to overloading. As described in Section 2.5.2, there are few cases of overloading in current versions of Miranda, and these are handled by various special tricks.

A class can be thought of as a collection of types which share some property. This property allows certain operators or functions to be overloaded by being defined on all the types in the class. When a class is declared, the operators and functions which are to be defined on all the types in that class are specified. When a type is declared as belonging to a particular class, the operators and functions of the class are defined on that type.

For example, a few of the many standard classes of Haskell, together with the relationships between them, can be pictured as:

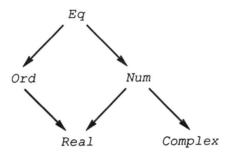

The class *Eq* consists of all types for which values can be compared for equality. This includes most data types, but excludes functions. Whenever a type is declared as belonging to this class, it must have the equality testing operator, which is == in Haskell, defined on it. There is a default implementation of ==, but the programmer has the choice of redefining it.

The class *Eq* contains a subclass *Ord* consisting of all ordered types, i.e. ones on which the comparison operators are defined, and a subclass *Num* of numerical types on which arithmetic operators are defined. The class *Num* is not a subclass of *Ord* because *Num* includes complex numbers of class *Complex* which have no natural linear ordering. On the other hand, the class *Real* of real numbers (which includes fixed and arbitrary precision integers, single and double precision floating point numbers, and rationals) is a subclass of both *Num* and *Ord*.

The programmer can define a new class, specify that a type belongs to a particular class (giving the definitions of the class operations for that type at the same time), and can specify class restrictions on the types of functions. For example, the natural type of a sorting function might be:

```
sort  ::  (Ord t)  =>  [t] -> [t]
```

This specifies that, for any ordered type *t*, the *sort* function has type *[t] -> [t]* (*t* is recognised as a type variable, like * in Miranda, because type names start with capital letters).

There are many more facilities provided for using classes, and they have an impact on many other features of the language. However, as with types, they are very unobtrusive most of the time.

There is still a lot of research being carried out into the design and implementation of functional languages, much of it in conjunction with the emergence of parallel computers, and we can look forward to many interesting developments in the future.

# Appendix A
# Miranda Session Commands

The information in Appendix A and Appendix B is based on release two of the Miranda system. I am grateful to Research Software Limited for permission to include this information.

A Miranda session is typically entered by giving an operating system command such as *mira*. There are a number of commands which can be given in a Miranda session, the most important of which are the following:

| | |
|---|---|
| *expr* | evaluate expression *expr* |
| *expr::* | find type of *expr* |
| | |
| */file name* | change current script to *name.m* |
| */edit* | edit current script |
| */quit* | end session |
| | |
| */help* | display main commands |
| */man* | enter online reference manual |
| */count* | switch on measurement of time/space |

# Appendix B
# Some Standard Functions

The Miranda standard environment provides a useful library of standard functions and types, available for use in all expressions and scripts. Some of the more commonly used ones are summarised below in alphabetical order. The descriptions given here are not necessarily the same as those given in the Miranda standard environment. For full details and a complete list of Miranda standard functions the reader should consult the Miranda system manual. For convenience of reference the standard functions given here are preceded by a summary of Miranda's operators. These are given roughly in order of increasing precedence – for the exact precedence rules, see the Miranda system manual.

$\boxed{(:)}$ is an infix constructor for building a list by attaching a new member to the front. For example, the list $[1,2]$ can be represented as $1:2:[]$, which is short for $1:(2:[])$. The list type is built in, but is an algebraic type which acts as if defined by:

```
[*]   ::=   [] | *:[*]
```

$\boxed{(++)}$ is an infix operator for joining two lists, so $"car" ++ "pet"$ is $"carpet"$. It acts as if defined by:

```
[] ++ ys   =   ys
(x:rxs) ++ ys   =   x : (rxs ++ ys)
```

$\boxed{(--)}$ is an infix operator which removes from a list the first occurrence, if any, of each member of a second list, so $[1,2,3] -- [2,4]$ is $[1,3]$. It acts as if defined by:

```
xs -- []  =  xs
xs -- (y:rys)
=  (remove y xs) -- rys  where
   remove y []  =  []
   remove y (x:rxs)
   =  rxs,                     if x=y
   =  x : remove y rxs,  otherwise
```

$\boxed{(\backslash/)}$ is an infix boolean 'or' operator. It acts as if defined by:

```
False \/ b  =  b
True \/ b  =  True
```

$\boxed{(\&)}$ is an infix boolean 'and' operator. It acts as if defined by:

```
False & b  =  False
True & b  =  b
```

$\boxed{(\sim)}$ is a prefix boolean 'not' operator. It acts as if defined by:

```
~ False  =  True
~ True  =  False
```

$\boxed{(>),\ (>=),\ (=),\ (\sim=),\ (<=)\ \text{and}\ (<)}$ are infix comparison operators.
They are overloaded – they work on all data types by comparing constructors, and then each field in turn. For example, they work on the list constructors as if defined by:

```
[] < []  =  False
[] < (y:rys)  =  True
(x:rxs) < []  =  False
(x:rxs) < (y:rys)  =  (x<y) \/ (x=y & rxs<rys)
...
```

$\boxed{(+),\ (-),\ (*)\ \text{and}\ (/)}$ are infix numerical operators which work on integers and floating point numbers. If applied to an integer and a floating point
number, the integer is converted to floating point first. The – operator is
also used as a prefix negation operator.

$\boxed{(div)}$ is an infix integer division operator. It works as if defined using
*entier*, except that it only works on integers, and it works for integers of
any precision:

$$n \; \textbf{div} \; m \; = \; entier \; (n/m)$$

$(mod)$ is an infix integer remainder operator. Both arguments must be integers, and it works as if defined by:

$$n \; \textbf{mod} \; m \; = \; n \; - \; m \; * \; (n \; \textbf{div} \; m)$$

$(\char`\^)$ is an infix exponentiation operator which works on integers and floating point numbers.

$(.)$ is an infix operator which composes two functions, so that $f.g$ is a combined function which, when applied to $x$, gives $f \; (g \; x)$. It works as if defined by:

$$(f.g) \; x \; = \; f \; (g \; x)$$

$(\#)$ is a prefix operator for finding the length of a list, as if defined by:

```
# []    =  0
# (x:rxs)   =  1 + #rxs
```

$(!)$ is an infix operator for extracting a member from a given position in a list. Its second argument must be an integer, but otherwise it works as if defined by:

```
[] ! n   =  error "subscript out of range"
(x:rxs) ! 0  =  x
(x:rxs) ! (n+1)   =  rxs!n
```

$(\$f)$ is an infix operator corresponding to the function $f$. This works as if each identifier representing a function or constructor has a corresponding operator defined by:

$$x \; \$f \; y \; = \; f \; x \; y$$

$and$ takes a list of booleans and checks whether they are all $True$:

$$and \; bs \; = \; foldr \; (\&) \; True \; bs$$

$bool$ is the built-in boolean type. It is enumerated, as if defined by:

$$bool \; ::= \; False \; | \; True$$

$\boxed{char}$ is the built-in character type containing all the characters that can be typed on a keyboard. It is an enumerated type, as if defined by:

    char   ::=   '\0' | '\1' | '\2' | ...

$\boxed{concat}$ joins a list of lists together into a single list. Two possible definitions are shown:

    concat xss   =   foldr (++) [] xss

    OR   concat xss   =   [x | xs<-xss; x<-xs]

$\boxed{drop}$ removes a given number of items from the beginning of a list. If the list has less than the required number of members, *drop* returns *[]*. The first argument must be an integer:

    drop 0 xs   =   xs
    drop (n+1) []   =   []
    drop (n+1) (x:rxs)   =   drop n rxs

$\boxed{dropwhile}$ removes items from the front of a list while a given test is satisfied:

    dropwhile f []   =   []
    dropwhile f (x:rxs)
    =   dropwhile f rxs,   **if f x**
    =   x:rxs,             **otherwise**

$\boxed{error}$ is a built-in function which stops a program with a given error message when it is evaluated.

$\boxed{filter}$ finds those members of a list which pass a given test:

    filter f xs   =   [x | x<-xs; f x]

$\boxed{foldl}$ folds up a list from the left, using a given binary operator and a given starting value. Thus *foldl op c [x,y,z,...]* is equal to *((c $op x) $op y) $op z....* It can be thought of as running through the list forming a "running total". To ensure that this total takes up constant space, rather than expanding as an unevaluated expression, *foldl* has a built-in implementation in which the second argument is evaluated before each call. In the definition given here, *seq* is a function which (head) evaluates its first argument and then returns its second:

```
foldl op c []  =  c
foldl op c (x:rxs)
= seq c (foldl op (c $op x) rxs)
```

`foldll` is similar to `foldl` except that it only applies to non-empty lists, and uses the first member to initialise the running total:

```
foldll op []  =  error "foldll applied to []"
foldll op (x:rxs)  =  foldl op x rxs
```

`foldr` folds up a list from the right, using a given binary operator and a given starting value. Thus `foldr op c [x,y,z,...]` is equal to $x$ `$op` ($y$ `$op` ($z$ ... `$op` $c$)):

```
foldr op c []  =  c
foldr op c (x:rxs)  =  x $op (foldr op c rxs)
```

`foldrl` is similar to `foldr` except that it takes a non-empty list and has no starting value:

```
foldrl op []  =  error "foldrl applied to []"
foldrl op [x]  =  x
foldrl op (x:rxs)  =  x $op (foldrl op rxs)
```

`fst` returns the first component of a pair:

```
fst (x,y) = x
```

`hd` returns the first member of a list:

```
hd []  =  error "hd of []"
hd (x:rxs)  =  x
```

`id` is the identity function which returns its argument unchanged:

```
id x  =  x
```

`init` removes the last member from a list:

```
init []  =  error "init of []"
init [x]  =  []
init (x:rxs)  =  x : init rxs
```

$\boxed{iterate}$ takes a function and an initial value and returns the infinite list which results from applying $f$ repeatedly, starting with the given initial value:

$$iterate\ f\ x\ =\ x\ :\ iterate\ f\ (f\ x)$$

$\boxed{last}$ finds the last member of a list:

$$last\ xs\ =\ xs!(\#xs-1)$$

$\boxed{map}$ applies a given function to every member of a list:

$$map\ f\ xs\ =\ [f\ x\ |\ x<-xs]$$

$\boxed{map2}$ applies a given function of two arguments to each pair of corresponding members taken from two given lists:

$$map2\ f\ xs\ ys\ =\ [f\ x\ y\ |\ (x,y)\ <-\ zip2\ xs\ ys]$$

$\boxed{max}$ finds the largest member in a given list:

$$max\ xs\ =\ foldl1\ max2\ xs$$

$\boxed{max2}$ finds the larger of two values:

$$max2\ x\ y$$
$$=\ x,\ \ if\ x>=y$$
$$=\ y,\ \ otherwise$$

$\boxed{member}$ tests whether a given item is in a given list:

$$member\ xs\ y\ =\ or\ [x=y\ |\ x<-xs]$$

$\boxed{num}$ is the built-in type consisting of integers and fixed precision floating point numbers.

$\boxed{or}$ takes a list of booleans and checks whether at least one of them is $True$:

$$or\ bs\ =\ foldr\ (\backslash/)\ False\ bs$$

$\boxed{product}$ finds the product of a list of numbers:

$$product\ ns\ =\ foldl\ (*)\ 1\ ns$$

$\boxed{read}$ is a built-in function which returns the contents of a file with a given name as a stream of characters.

$\boxed{repeat}$ forms an infinite list by repeating a given value indefinitely. The second of the two definitions given here is more efficient:

```
repeat x  =  x : repeat x

OR  repeat x  =  xs  where  xs  =  x:xs
```

$\boxed{reverse}$ reverses the order of the members of a list:

```
reverse xs
=  foldl join [] xs  where
       join ys y  =  y:ys
```

$\boxed{scan}$ produces a list of "running totals" by using a given operator to incorporate each member of a given list in turn into a given initial total. It can also be used interactively to produce a stream of states from a given stream of commands (see Chapter 5). In that case, it is important that $c$ should be returned as the first member of the result before pattern matching is used on $xs$:

```
scan op c xs
=  c : step xs  where
       step []  =  []
       step (x:rxs)  =  scan op (c $op x) rxs
```

$\boxed{show}$ is a built-in overloaded function for converting values into a textual form suitable for display. It actually represents a family of functions, one for each type.

$\boxed{snd}$ returns the second item in a given pair:

```
snd (x,y)  =  y
```

$\boxed{sort}$ is a function which sorts a given list into order. The definition given here uses the quick sort algorithm, using the middle member as the pivot:

```
sort []  =  []
```

```
sort xs
=   ys ++ [x | x<-xs; x=pivot] ++ zs
    where
    pivot  =  xs ! (#xs div 2)
    ys  =  sort [x | x<-xs; x<pivot]
    zs  =  sort [x | x<-xs; x>pivot]
```

sum finds the sum of a list of numbers:

```
sum ns  =   foldl (+) 0 ns
```

take is a function which returns a given number of items from the beginning of a given list. If the list has less than the required number of members, *take* returns as many as possible. The first argument must be an integer:

```
take 0 xs  =  []
take (n+1) []  =  []
take (n+1) (x:rxs)  =  x : take n rxs
```

takewhile returns items from the front of a given list, while a given test is satisfied:

```
takewhile f []  =  []
takewhile f (x:rxs)
=   x : takewhile f rxs,    if f x
=   [],                     otherwise
```

tl removes the first member of a list:

```
tl []  =  error "tl of []"
tl (x:rxs)  =  rxs
```

undef stops a program with an *"undefined"* error message:

```
undef  =  error "undefined"
```

until is a loop function which applies a function *g* repeatedly to a value *x* until a given test *f* succeeds:

```
until f g x
=   x,                      if f x
=   until f g (g x),        otherwise
```

| `zip2`, `zip3`, `zip4`, `zip5` and `zip6` | take a number of lists and return a single list of corresponding tuples. The result list is equal in length to the shortest of the original lists. The definitions of `zip2` and `zip3` are illustrated here:

```
zip2 (x:rxs) (y:rys)  =  (x,y) : zip2 rxs rys
zip2 xs ys  =  []

zip3 (x:rxs) (y:rys) (z:rzs)
=  (x,y,z) : zip3 rxs rys rzs
zip3 xs ys zs  =  []
```

# Bibliography

[1] Abramsky & Hankin (eds), *Abstract Interpretation of Declarative Languages*, Ellis Horwood 1987.

[2] Aho & Ullman, *Principles of Compiler Design*, Addison Wesley 1979.

[3] Aho, Hopcroft & Ullman, *Data Structures and Algorithms*, Addison Wesley 1983.

[4] Barendregt, *The Lambda Calculus – Its Syntax and Semantics*, North-Holland 1981.

[5] Bird & Wadler, *Introduction to Functional Programming*, Prentice Hall 1988.

[6] Field & Harrison, *Functional Programming*, Addison Wesley 1988.

[7] Jones, *Systematic Software Development Using VDM*, 2nd edition, Prentice Hall 1990.

[8] Jonkers, *A Fast Garbage Compaction Algorithm*, in *Information Processing Letters*, volume 9, number 1, 1979.

[9] Peyton Jones, *The Implementation of Functional Programming Languages*, Prentice Hall 1987.

[10] Peyton Jones & Salkild, *The spineless tagless G-machine*, in *Functional Programming and Computer Architecture*, proceedings of the 1989 ACM conference, Addison Wesley 1989.

[11] Research Software Limited, *The Miranda System Manual*, 1987, 1989.

[12] Schmidt, *Denotational Semantics: a Methodology for Program Development*, Allyn and Bacon, 1986.

[13] Sedgewick, *Algorithms*, 2nd edition, Addison Wesley 1988.

[14] Spivey, *The Z Notation*, Prentice Hall 1989.

[15] Sterling & Shapiro, *The Art of Prolog*, MIT Press 1986.

[16] D. Turner, *Miranda: A Non-Strict Functional Language with Polymorphic Types*, Proceedings, Functional Programming Languages and Computer Architecture 1985 (Springer-Verlag LNCS vol. 201)

[17] D. Turner, *An Overview of Miranda*, SIGPLAN Notices, vol. 21, no. 12, 1986

[18] R. Turner, *Constructive Foundations for Functional Languages*, McGraw-Hill 1991.

[19] Wikström, *Functional Programming Using Standard ML*, Prentice Hall 1987.

[20] Winston & Horn, *Lisp*, Addison Wesley 1981.

[21] *The Haskell Report*, available from either of these addresses:

```
The Haskell Project          The Haskell Project
Dept. of Computing Science   Dept. of Computer Science
University of Glasgow        Yale University
Glasgow                      Box 2158 Yale Station
G12 8QQ                      New Haven CT 06520
SCOTLAND                     USA
```

# Index